ASIA SMALL AND MEDIUM-SIZED ENTERPRISE MONITOR 2021

VOLUME III—DIGITALIZING MICROFINANCE IN BANGLADESH: FINDINGS FROM THE BASELINE SURVEY

APRIL 2022

ASIAN DEVELOPMENT BANK

ADB

© 2022 Asian Development Bank
6 ADB Avenue, Mandaluyong City, 1550 Metro Manila, Philippines
Tel +63 2 8632 4444; Fax +63 2 8636 2444
www.adb.org

Some rights reserved. Published in 2022.

ISBN 978-92-9269-477-7 (print); 978-92-9269-478-4 (electronic); 978-92-9269-479-1 (ebook)
Publication Stock No. TCS220161-2
DOI: http://dx.doi.org/10.22617/TCS220161-2

The views expressed in this publication are those of the authors and do not necessarily reflect the views and policies of the Asian Development Bank (ADB) or its Board of Governors or the governments they represent.

ADB does not guarantee the accuracy of the data included in this publication and accepts no responsibility for any consequence of their use. The mention of specific companies or products of manufacturers does not imply that they are endorsed or recommended by ADB in preference to others of a similar nature that are not mentioned.

By making any designation of or reference to a particular territory or geographic area, or by using the term "country" in this document, ADB does not intend to make any judgments as to the legal or other status of any territory or area.

Please contact pubsmarketing@adb.org if you have questions or comments with respect to content, or if you wish to obtain copyright permission for your intended use that does not fall within these terms, or for permission to use the ADB logo.

Corrigenda to ADB publications may be found at http://www.adb.org/publications/corrigenda.

Notes:
In this publication, "$" refers to United States dollars and "Tk" refers to taka.
ADB recognizes "China" as the People's Republic of China.

Cover design by Claudette Rodrigo.

Printed on recycled paper

Contents

Tables and Figures

Foreword

Limited access to formal financial services is a chronic problem that impedes the growth of micro, small, and medium-sized enterprises (MSMEs) in any country. Governments have provided intensive financial assistance programs to MSMEs during the coronavirus disease (COVID-19) pandemic through debt restructuring, special refinancing schemes, and credit guarantees, which helped improve their access to bank credit. However, financing constraints remain high in many MSMEs in developing Asia. In the nonbank financial sector, it is hoped that microfinance institutions can fill the unmet financing demand from smaller firms and entrepreneurs. Given the post-COVID-19 economy that promotes contactless societies, digital transformation should be further encouraged for businesses, including the microfinance industry.

This thematic third volume of the *Asia Small and Medium-Sized Enterprise Monitor (ASM) 2021* focuses on the digitalization of microfinance in Bangladesh. The study aims to assess how the financial services of microfinance institutions can be digitalized to help boost growth among smaller firms and entrepreneurs by using an impact evaluation approach.

The Asian Development Bank partnered with the Bangladesh Institute of Development Studies to conduct the baseline study. The field survey was disrupted by surging COVID-19 cases and subsequent lockdowns in Bangladesh. Yet, the team was able to complete the baseline survey in late December 2021 despite these difficult conditions and prepared the report in early 2022. The study was financed by the Japan Fund for Prosperous and Resilient Asia and the Pacific as part of the ASM project.

The study offers justification to pilot a full-scale randomized controlled trial to assess the effects of a digitalized version of a group-based credit scheme that can expand financial services to smaller firms at an affordable price. We hope this report and ongoing studies facilitate our member governments' discussions on the digitalization of microfinance in the post-COVID-19 economy.

Albert Park
Chief Economist and Director General
Economic Research and Regional Cooperation Department
Asian Development Bank

Acknowledgments

The *Asia Small and Medium-Sized Enterprise Monitor (ASM) 2021, Volume III—Digitalizing Microfinance in Bangladesh: Findings from the Baseline Survey* was prepared by the thematic study subteam of the ASM, comprising the subject experts listed below. The thematic study was led, reviewed, and edited by Shigehiro Shinozaki, senior economist, Economic Research and Regional Cooperation Department (ERCD) of the Asian Development Bank (ADB). The report was authored by Shahid Khandker, ADB consultant; Minhaj Mahmud, ADB consultant; and Hussain Samad, ADB consultant. The research was assisted by Ahmed Adib, Rezoanul Haque, and Mashiat Hoque at the Bangladesh Institute of Development Studies (BIDS). The study was jointly implemented under technical assistance (TA) 9746-REG: Upgrading the Asia Small and Medium-Sized Enterprise Monitor and TA 6585-REG: Impact Evaluation of Financial Technology Innovations in Selected Developing Member Countries. The study benefited from the advice and inputs of Takashi Yamano, principal economist of the Economic Analysis and Operational Support Division, ERCD.

The baseline survey was implemented by Dhaka-based thinktank BIDS from October to December 2021. In this study, we faced serious difficulty in conducting field surveys because of surging COVID-19 cases and mobility restrictions in Bangladesh at the time. Against this backdrop, we completed the baseline survey, although we were forced to reschedule the planned publication to 2022. This study was funded by the Japan Fund for Poverty Reduction as cofinancing partner to the ASM project. Administrative support was provided by Richard Supangan and Maria Frederika Bautista.

Shahid Khandker is a development economist with research experience over 30 years at the World Bank and other development organizations. He was a lead economist at the World Bank's Development Research Group. After his retirement from the World Bank in 2015, he spent more than 2 years as a visiting senior research fellow at the International Food Policy Research Institute. He has been a leading researcher in the areas of microfinance, rural and agri-finance, poverty, gender, and rural infrastructural development. He is a micro-econometrician with 30 years of experience in household survey design, micro-data collection, and analysis.

Minhaj Mahmud recently joined ADB as a senior economist at ERCD. Before joining ADB, he was a senior research fellow at the BIDS and worked as ADB consultant for this study. He serves in the editorial board of the Journal of International Development (Wiley's). His field of research is broadly behavioral economics and development economics, with a focus on field experiments and impact evaluation in health, education, labor, gender, climate change, and political economy issues. He holds a doctor of philosophy (PhD) degree in economics from the University of Gothenburg in Sweden.

Hussain Samad, in a career of over 25 years in the development sector, has worked for major development organizations including the World Bank, ADB, JICA, Inter-American Development Bank, and International Food Policy Research Institute. He has managed research projects; provided technical support to regions; overseen data collection activities; and authored books, articles, and reports. His skill set includes impact evaluation;

policy analysis; survey, sampling, and questionnaire design; and advanced data analysis. He has a master's degree from Northeastern University in the United States.

Shigehiro Shinozaki is a senior economist at ERCD, ADB. His advisory and research expertise includes policy issues in small and medium-sized enterprise development, inclusive finance, and financial sector development, especially in developing Asia. He has held several expert positions, including as a special officer for development finance at Japan's Ministry of Finance, an advisor to the Indonesian Capital Market and Financial Institution Supervisory Agency as a JICA expert, and an administrator at the Organisation for Economic Co-operation and Development. He holds a PhD in international studies from Waseda University in Japan.

Abbreviations

ADB	–	Asian Development Bank
BIDS	–	Bangladesh Institute of Development Studies
BSCIC	–	Bangladesh Small and Cottage Industries Corporation
CMSME	–	cottage, micro, small, and medium-sized enterprise
COVID-19	–	coronavirus disease
ERCD	–	Economic Research and Regional Cooperation Department
HIES	–	Household Income and Expenditure Survey
MFI	–	microfinance institution
MFS	–	mobile financial services
MRA	–	Microcredit Regulatory Authority
MSME	–	micro, small, and medium-sized enterprise
NBFI	–	nonbank finance institution
NGO	–	nongovernment organization
PKSF	–	Palli Karma Sahayak Foundation
RCT	–	randomized controlled trial
ROA	–	return on assets
SDG	–	Sustainable Development Goal

Executive Summary

In Bangladesh, micro, small, and medium-sized enterprises (MSMEs), which constitute 99.97% of all industries and absorb 86% of the labor force, have huge potential for employment creation and income generation (Asian Development Bank 2021). MSMEs contribute 25% to the country's gross domestic product (GDP), and the government's target is for this to reach 32% by 2024. However, access to affordable finance has remained a big hurdle to reaching this goal. While microfinance institutions (MFIs) provide more than 50% of their loan portfolios to support MSMEs, their transaction costs are high. One option to make MFIs affordable, which is being increasingly considered, is to digitalize microfinance lending.

A baseline study was carried out from October to December 2021 to pilot a randomized controlled trial intervention to determine whether digitalized microfinance can be introduced at an affordable price. The baseline study addresses a number of issues related to MSMEs: their inputs, outputs, and productivity; access to microfinance; and exposure to shocks including the coronavirus disease (COVID-19) pandemic. Based on the poverty map of the country from the 2016 Household Income and Expenditure Survey (HIES), a sample frame was developed with some 24,000 households from 124 villages in 5 districts in the impoverished Rangpur division of Bangladesh. About 3,000 households were randomly sampled, keeping the proportionality of MFI participation and MSME households from the census (sampling frame).

On average, 42.5% of surveyed household heads have no education at all, and only 7.6% have completed higher secondary education and above. Furthermore, 78.2% of the households are functionally landless (owning less than 0.5 acre of land), with only 2.4% households being medium to large landholders (owning 2.5 acres or more). The majority of household heads are self-employed in the farm sector (42%), followed by wage employment (40%). About 32% of households are involved in MSME activities. Among them, about 52% are engaged in services, about 43% in trading, and only about 5% in manufacturing.

MSME households are better off than non-MSME households, enjoying at least three times the income of an average non-MSME household. MSMEs dominate the rural nonfarm sector—66% of the nonfarm income and 49% of total household income are drawn from MSME activities. Owned and operated mostly by men (96%) and with majority of them having primary-level education or less, MSME activities use very little hired labor (22%). The enterprises have been in operation for an average of 9 years, are mostly household-based (58%), and only 27% of them are registered.

Over 70% of the MSME households have access to microcredit, while only 20% reported having access to formal banks. Nearly 80% of the MSME households also use mobile financial services (MFS). Overall, about 93% of the surveyed households have access to at least one of these sources. However, the startup capital of these enterprises comes primarily from their own savings or the support of family members (56%). About 35% of the surveyed MSMEs' activities are supported by microcredit loans.

MSME activities are profitable, with the return on assets being as high as 53% for some MSMEs. The average rate of return on capital or assets is 38% when a production function is used, and 22% when a profit function is estimated. MSME activities vary in productivity by access to finance—revenue, profits, and rates of return are much higher for those with access to finance than for those without such access. MFI participation increases MSME revenue by 4.2%, on average, without affecting MSME net profit, above and beyond what is accounted for by capital and other factors. On the other hand, MFS participation does not seem to have any statistically significant effect on revenue or profit.

The extent of credit constraints is low at only 5.6% among MSME entrepreneurs. Nonetheless, credit constraints seem to impede productivity—revenue, profits, and rates of return for credit-constrained MSMEs are all lower than those of unconstrained MSMEs.

Besides looking at MSME productivity, the study also examined the role of access to finance in overall household income. Econometric analysis suggests that MFI participation increases household nonfarm income by 5%, farm income by 4%, and total income by 9%. Results also suggest a modest income gain from joint participation in an MFI or MFS for non-MSME households.

COVID-19 has impacted MSME productivity in Bangladesh. The survey found that a COVID-19 outbreak in a village caused at least a 20% profit loss for MSME activities in that village. In fact, MSME households lost more income and employment due to the impacts of COVID-19 than non-MSME households. Findings also suggest that government and nongovernment stimulus did not reach them adequately or was not effective. Many households had to reduce consumption or use savings to weather the pandemic.

Findings from the baseline study provide justification for further study on the digitalization of microfinance. The aim is to assess how the financial services of MFIs can be digitalized to help boost growth in the MSME sector, which provides the lion's share of rural income in Bangladesh. As MFIs largely support MSME activities, they could be much more affordable if their services were digitalized. Given MFS have been the fastest way of transferring money via cashless transfer mechanisms, it remains to be seen if MFI operations, including lending, can be digitalized and if so, what it would mean in terms of productivity gains and income growth in the MSME sector.

1. Introduction

This report is based on a baseline survey for the purpose of a randomized controlled trial (RCT) on the scope of the digitalization of microfinance in support of microenterprise growth in Bangladesh, with the objective of evaluating financial technology innovations and how financial innovations can help alleviate suffering during the coronavirus disease (COVID-19) pandemic. The objective of this study is to assess (i) the benefits of rural microenterprises in terms of income and productivity, and (ii) the role of microfinance in supporting microenterprise growth in Bangladesh.

Digital financial services have been introduced in recent years to work via web, mobile, and cloud services, among other ways. The most common type of digital financial services in Bangladesh are mobile financial services (MFS), which rely on mobile phone technology to deliver secured, fast, and inexpensive financial transactions such as payments and money transfers. MFS are generally characterized by low marginal costs per account or transaction and can therefore bring efficiencies of scale and cost reduction in financial transactions.

As mobile technology has the potential to enhance the efficiency of group-based credit and savings services for the poor, it is possible that integrating mobile phone technology, in particular MFS, into the financial transactions of microfinance institutions (MFIs) in Bangladesh, who support the poor's income-generating activities, can save time and money in loan disbursement and collection, cash management, document processing, and verification of potential clients. Consequently, branch operations and staff activities are likely to be more efficient. If much of the cost savings can be transferred to clients, with the likelihood of interest rates being decreased, it is expected that digitalization of microfinance operations could be a win–win scenario for the providers and clients alike. Microfinance supports mostly rural microenterprises, also known as rural nonfarm activities (Khandker et al. 2016). Digitalization of microfinance can thus enhance productivity and growth more effectively in micro, small, and medium-sized enterprises (MSMEs), which currently dominate output and employment in the nonfarm rural sector of Bangladesh.

According to the Bangladesh Household Income and Expenditure Survey (HIES) of 2016, 59% of the income of rural households comes from the nonfarm sector: 33% from non-agriculture wages; 11% from non-agriculture self-employment; and the remaining 15% from rental, remittance (domestic and foreign), transfers, and so on. The same survey finds that the share of employment among rural households in the nonfarm sector is 51%. On the other hand, the 2013 Economic Census and the 2013 Enterprise Survey reveal that 99% of all nonfarm enterprises in Bangladesh were in the micro and small categories, and they provided employment to 20% of the population of 160 million (World Bank 2019).

Inadequate access to finance for MSMEs is a major barrier to the development of the MSME sector and its contribution to the overall financial and economic development of the country. MFIs in Bangladesh in general support six broad types of loans: (i) microcredit for self-employed activities, (ii) microenterprise loans, (iii) loans for the ultra-poor, (iv) agricultural loans, (v) seasonal loans, and (vi) loans for disaster management. Loans up to Tk50,000 are generally considered microcredit, while those of more than Tk50,000 but below Tk1 million are considered microenterprise loans.

While MFIs are major sources of credit for microenterprises, funding is observed to be inadequate to meet demand. The economic slowdown due to the COVID-19 pandemic over the last 2 years has perhaps worsened the situation and limited microenterprises' access to finance. Like many other economic sectors in Bangladesh, microfinance was not spared during the pandemic, which severely affected microfinance customers and service providers alike. During the peak of the lockdown, the activities supported by microcredit were affected in a number of ways. First and foremost, customers of microfinance products and services—who are a vulnerable segment of the population to begin with—lost their job or their income was reduced, limiting their ability to consume such products and services. Second, lockdowns disrupted the country's supply chains, which affected microfinance customers' ability to carry out their income-generating activities. Restricted supply chains also raised the price of consumer goods in general, affecting everybody, including microfinance borrowers.

These constraints also decreased their ability to repay microloans, resulting in increased loan defaults. Because of reduced loan disbursements and collections, MFI operations also suffered, many branches were closed down and many MFI staffs lost their jobs. Thus, COVID-19 had a spiraling effect on both the borrowers and service providers of microfinance. To mitigate the crisis, the government offered a range of stimulus packages for microenterprises, with a total amount of $1.2 billion. However, the amount was not enough for the large demand for funding from microenterprises. It was estimated that MFIs needed at least an additional $2.2 billion (ADB 2021).

Microenterprises, generally defined as those activities employing 1–9 people, dominate the rural nonfarm sector in Bangladesh—about 98% of rural nonfarm activities are microenterprises. As per the projection of the country's largest on-lending funding agency of microfinance, Palli Karma Sahayak Foundation (PKSF), $170 million of additional financing was deemed necessary for post-COVID-19 economic recovery to meet microenterprises' demand for working capital. It is an open issue to determine if MFIs and borrowers managed (and, if so, how) to cope with the negative consequences of this historical global health shock. In general, while the Government of Bangladesh provided payouts for vulnerable populations, the amount was modest and mostly included a one-time transfer payment. However, MFIs in Bangladesh showed resilience in the past by supporting their borrowers with emergency or disaster loans, loan moratoriums, and other schemes such as training programs on coping strategies. It is an important research question to determine to what extent government assistance was provided and how successful it was in mitigating the crisis in the MSME and MFI sectors.

This study addresses several related issues surrounding microfinance, MSMEs, and COVID-19. In order to study these interlinked issues, baseline data collection was carried out during October–December 2021. The purpose of this baseline is to help design an RCT study to assess how a digitalized version of microfinance can be a win–win situation for both MFIs and MSMEs. However, the data collected were for households engaged in microenterprises, as well as other rural activities including farming, and for branch-level information of MFIs serving these households. The data therefore have the potential to facilitate investigation of a number of outstanding related issues: (i) how MFI borrowers were affected by the COVID-19 pandemic health-wise and economically; (ii) how their microfinance transactions were affected (receiving loans, repayments, and savings); (iii) how their income-generating activities, which are supported by MFIs, were affected; (iv) how MFI branch activities were affected by COVID-19; (v) whether MFI borrowers utilize MFS services to secure and repay loans or deposit savings; and (vi) whether microenterprises received any stimulus money offered by the government or the MFI on-lending agencies. Moreover, the scope of this data collection under the baseline survey is to facilitate examining how MFI operations were likewise affected by the pandemic and whether they received any stimulus money for their expected losses in loan collection and savings mobilization due to COVID-19.

Our approach in this study is consistent with a large literature on the subject of access to finance and its role in microenterprise growth. A large body of literature has already documented that better access to affordable finance (in terms of better terms and conditions of loans as well as reliable source) is essential for improved productivity and growth in any economy (e.g., Butler and Cornaggia 2011, Cull and Xu 2005, Sawada and Zhang 212, Wang 2008). In fact, while other obstacles matter, a lack of access to finance consistently emerges as the single most important and robust factor constraining firm enterprise growth (e.g., Aterido et al. 2011, Beck et al. 2006, Beck et al. 2005, Buyinza and Bbaale 2013, Deininger and Jin 2007, de Mel et al. 2008, Rand 2007).

Our study uses baseline data collected from households, communities, and MFI branches active in the study villages. Data analysis confirms some stylized facts. Microenterprise dominates the rural nonfarm sector in terms of income—more than 90% of nonfarm income and about 70% of total household income is drawn from MSME activities. MSMEs consist of cottage and small manufacturing and other businesses and services that play an important role in the rural economy. Startup capital for these enterprises comes primarily from their own savings or the support of family members—not from banks or even MFIs. However, MFIs extend support to existing MSMEs— they lend about 45% of their loan portfolios to MSMEs once they have been established using their own resources.

Credit constraint is found to be an important factor for explaining lower returns to productivity. Nonetheless, the estimated rate of return to capital is about 20%. Many MFIs charge more than 20% interest for loans extended to microenterprises. The banks charge less than 15% interest (more recently, about 10%) and often extend a loan beyond 1 year, whereas the average duration of an MFI loan is 1 year. Banks are reluctant to finance MSMEs despite the fact that loan recovery rates are observed to be more than 95%. (The loan recovery rate was close to 90% even during the pandemic.) However, pandemic-related stimulus did not reach most of these enterprises and, on average, they lost as much as 20% of their income during this period.

While as much as 70% of rural households have MFS membership, their (MFS) impact on enterprise productivity is not much. On the other hand, as microenterprises depend on microfinance (they draw more than 60% of their loans from MFIs), there is merit for digitalizing microfinance. This is justified for a number of reasons such as the cashless and speedy transfer of money. But a very small percentage of MSME households (about 4%) are found to use MFS to pay loans or deposit money as savings, although digitalizing lending of MFIs has not been yet introduced for their clients. Hence, there is scope for an experimental research design evaluating whether and how microfinance lending (as well as savings and loan repayment and insurance) can be digitalized. The baseline study design to study this question is therefore justified on this ground.

The report is organized as follows. Section 2 discusses the survey design and salient features of the data collected from three major stakeholders of MSMEs: (i) households that are engaged in MSME activities as compared with those who are not—MSMEs are largely cottage and small enterprises employing up to 10 persons (household survey); (ii) MFIs supporting these enterprises (MFI survey); and (iii) communities where these households and enterprises are situated (community survey). This section also discusses the sampling frame for data collection, which was the basis for the random drawing of 124 surveyed villages (communities), 2,993 households, and 285 MFI branches.

Section 3 discusses how the MSME sector is defined and its current state, both in terms of coverage and sector distribution in Bangladesh, as per government statistics such as the latest round of the Economic Census of 2013 and different rounds of the HIES. It also discusses the financing and regulatory authorities governing the sector's performance.

Section 4 presents and discusses the trend of microfinance growth in terms of outreach (measured by membership and loan disbursement, and savings mobilized), and financial efficiency indicators (profitability and interest rates on lending and savings) using aggregate time-series national-level as well as branch-level data of the three largest MFIs covering some 80% of MFI transactions. Branch-level data permits a comparison of MFI performance before and after COVID-19 hit the economy and impacted the MSME sector.

Section 5 discusses the alternative sources of finance to MSMEs. The financial services consist of four major sources—banks, MFIs, MFS, and informal finance. Data show that the largest sources of MSME finance are MFIs and MFS. While MFIs are an outlet for MSMEs to save and borrow, MFS are the only source for transferring money for different purposes; they are used to remit and receive money. Less than 1% of MFI users use MFS to repay loans and save money. Analysis of household- and enterprise-level data shows that as much as 70% of households and 80% of MSME owners have both MFI and MFS accounts.

Section 6 discusses the sources of startup capital and estimates rates of return to capital for all three categories of microenterprises. It also examines the role of improved access to financial services in MSME productivity and income. Both financial accounting data and a production function approach is used to estimate the return on assets (ROA). Results are encouraging—returns to capital are as high as 37% and as low as 22%. Despite such high returns to investment for MSMEs, commercial banks are reluctant to finance them—only 19% of MSMEs have an account with banks. In contrast, MSME access to MFIs is as high as 60%. Yet, MSMEs are credit constrained and thus the question remains of how to provide capital at affordable prices to MSMEs. Banks charge about a 9% rate of interest against loans extended for a period longer than 1 year, while MFIs extend loans at a rate of about 24% for a short duration (often 1 year). So, improved access to long-term loans with lower interest rates is a way to enhance productivity and growth in the MSME sector.

Section 7 estimates the role of microfinance beyond microenterprises. Households that are engaged in MSME activities are also often involved in other income-generating activities. Therefore, the role of microfinance cannot be limited to evaluating its impact on MSMEs only. Rather, the MFI role needs to be evaluated against overall income generation. This section precisely estimates the net effect of MFIs on household income from farm and nonfarm sources as well as on overall income. Findings support the fact that MFIs play a positive role in raising both farm and nonfarm income. MFIs' impact is significant on nonfarm income for MSME households and on farm income for non-MSME households.

Section 8 examines the extent of COVID-19's impact on microenterprise productivity. Data analysis shows that microenterprises were hit hard by the pandemic. Households engaged in MSME activities lost income and suffered unemployment more than those who were not engaged in MSME activities. Such findings contradict the government perception that stimulus money must have reached the target groups. In fact, the econometric analysis does not find any such impact from stimulus measures, nor does it find that MFIs played any role in mitigating the negative impact of COVID-19. The pandemic impacted MSME productivity adversely, which could not be mitigated by external forces such as government stimulus money.

Section 9 concludes the report with implications for the future study of the digitalization of microfinance. The baseline survey data analysis justifies undertaking future study that assesses how the financial services of MFIs can be digitalized to help boost growth in the MSME sector, which provides the lion's share of rural income in Bangladesh. As MFIs largely support MSME activities, it follows also that the way financial institutions, including commercial banks, currently operate is not of much use unless their services are digitalized.

2. Salient Features of Census, Household, and Village Sample

In this section, we briefly discuss some of the salient features of the baseline data we collected through a village census, household surveys, and MFI branch surveys. As part of the sampling framework of the study, we first conducted a census in 150 selected villages in five districts of the Rangpur division in Bangladesh. The region is regarded as the poorest in terms of headcount ratios according to the latest 2016 HIES conducted by the Bangladesh Bureau of Statistics (see **Figure A.1** in the Appendix). Later, from the census list of 124 villages we randomly draw 3,000 households for the baseline study, keeping proportionality of mainly MFI participation and microenterprise households.[1] In these selected regions, we also conduct MFI branch surveys among the MFIs who are reported to have been serving the census households. Also, we conduct key informant interviews in all the selected villages to understand village-level characteristics. We report detail information in the Appendix.

A total of 24,708 households participated in the census across all five districts. Most of these (31%) were four-member households, similar across all districts. More than 70% of household heads were in the age range of 31–60 years and this percentage is also consistent across all five districts. A majority (93%) of surveyed households were headed by men. More than 41% of household heads had no formal education, while 14.5% of the household heads had completed primary education. Less than 4% of household heads had tertiary education. Almost 63% of households have no landownership. This percentage is highest in Kurigram and Rangpur (both around 67%) and lowest in Lalmonirhat (57%). Most of the households (more than three out of every four) do not own or operate any enterprise. This percentage is the lowest for Kurigram villages (66%) while relatively similar (about 75% to 79%) for the other four districts. Wholesale and retail business are the most common type of business (13%) and this is similar across all districts, followed by transport and communication (5.7%), which is highest in Gaibandha (almost 8%) and lowest in Lalmonirhat (less than 4%).

Only about 17% of respondents reported that a household head or spouse has access to a bank account. Kurigram villages have the highest percentage (21%) and Gaibandha villages have the lowest (15%). According to census data, on average, 65% of households reported that a household head or spouse uses an MFS account, with the highest percentages in Gaibandha (75%) and the lowest in Rangpur (48%).

As observed in **Table 1**, 20.5% of census households in Dinajpur are members of Grameen Bank (GB) and at least one other MFI (e.g., BRAC, ASA, Proshika, and BURO). The corresponding figures are 10.9% in Gaibandha, 13.7% in Kurigram, 9.6% in Lalmonirhat, and 10.2% in Rangpur. The average (GB households) for all five districts is 13.1%. Also, 15.1%, 6.0%, and 7.5% of households, respectively, in Dinajpur, Gaibandha, and Kurigram have accounts with BRAC and at least one other MFI. In Lalmonirhat and Rangpur, it is 13.9% and 10.2%, respectively. On average, BRAC households comprised 11.3% of the total across surveyed districts.

---

[1] To complete the surveys within the time allotted and resources available, we dropped five villages when drawing 3,000 households for interviews, following our criteria.

Table 1: Census Household Distribution by Microcredit Participation and by District
(%) (N = 24,489)

Microcredit Participation	Dinajpur	Gaibandha	Kurigram	Lalmonirhat	Rangpur	All Districts
All GB households	20.5	10.9	13.7	9.6	10.2	13.1
All BRAC households	15.1	6.0	7.5	13.9	12.8	11.3
All ASA households	19.6	20.9	13.6	18.4	21.2	19.0
Other program households	11.0	8.4	13.6	11.8	11.4	11.1
GB-only households	13.1	8.2	11.2	6.6	7.5	9.2
BRAC-only households	8.8	4.3	5.0	9.9	8.9	7.5
ASA-only households	11.7	16.6	10.1	13.7	15.8	13.7
Other program-only households	6.3	6.2	9.6	8.3	8.0	7.6
Multiple program households	18.5	15.7	7.5	11.1	13.9	13.6
Household eligible and willing to participate	11.9	8.1	17.2	6.6	8.0	10.0
Household ineligible and willing to participate	5.9	2.0	3.1	2.6	1.6	3.0
Household not willing to participate	23.8	38.9	36.3	41.2	36.3	35.2

GB = Grameen Bank.

Source: Authors' calculations based on the ADB–BIDS Digital Microcredit Survey 2021.

In the case of ASA, the above figures are relatively higher than for BRAC in all five districts. On average, 19% of households have accounts with ASA and at least one other MFI. For GB, 6.6% of households in Lalmonirhat (the lowest) have accounts with GB only, whereas the number is 13.1% in Dinajpur (the highest). The average is 9.2%. The percentage of BRAC-only households is the highest in Lalmonirhat (9.9%) and the lowest in Gaibandha (4.3%). The share of ASA-only households is the highest in Gaibandha (16.6%) and lowest in Kurigram (10.1%). In Dinajpur, 18.5% of households have multiple MFI accounts. The corresponding percentages in Gaibandha, Kurigram, Lalmonirhat, and Rangpur are 15.7%, 7.5%, 11.1%, and 13.9%, respectively. On average, 10.0% of households are eligible and willing to participate in MFI lending, with the highest and lowest figures in Kurigram (17.2%) and Lalmonirhat (6.6%), respectively. On average, about 3% of the households are ineligible but willing to participate, and 35.2% of households are not willing to participate, with the highest and lowest percentages in Lalmonirhat (41.2%) and Dinajpur (23.8%).

Table 2 shows findings from the household survey and indicate that 19.1% of sample households have accounts with GB and at least one other MFI. The highest percentage is in Dinajpur (30.4%) and the lowest is in Lalmonirhat (14.2%). In the cases of BRAC and ASA, the average participation rates are 15.3% and 25.4%, respectively. The GB-only, BRAC-only, and ASA-only households are on average 11.9%, 9.2%, and 15.1%, respectively, in the sample. On average, 15.7% of households participate in more than one program. The share of microcredit nonparticipants is the highest in Kurigram (54.0%) and the lowest in Dinajpur (32.0%).

Table 2: Household Survey: Sample Household Distribution by Microcredit Participation
(%) (N = 2,993)

Microcredit Participation	Dinajpur	Gaibandha	Kurigram	Lalmonirhat	Rangpur	All Districts
All GB households	30.4	17.6	16.5	14.2	16.3	19.1
All BRAC households	20.7	13.7	10.0	13.8	17.1	15.3
All ASA households	25.5	34.1	15.9	21.0	28.4	25.4
Other program households	21.0	23.8	10.6	15.7	18.1	18.2
GB-only households	15.0	10.9	14.0	10.1	9.9	11.9
BRAC-only households	12.1	6.4	6.3	10.4	9.9	9.2
ASA-only households	8.9	19.9	12.9	15.2	18.1	15.1
Other program-only households	6.8	10.4	6.8	10.0	7.6	8.3
Multiple program households	25.2	19.9	5.9	9.1	16.6	15.7
Overall microcredit participation	68.0	67.5	46.0	54.7	62.2	60.3
Microcredit nonparticipants	32.0	32.5	54.0	45.3	37.8	39.7

GB = Grameen Bank.

Source: Authors' calculations based on the ADB–BIDS Digital Microcredit Survey 2021.

From **Table 3,** we see that 78.2% of the sample households are landless, with the highest and lowest percentages of landlessness in Rangpur (83.4%) and Dinajpur (67.2%), respectively. In addition, 9.4% of the sample households are marginal landholders, whereas the percentages for small, medium, and large holders are 10.0%, 2.2%, and 0.2%, respectively.

Table 3: Household Distribution by Agricultural Landholding by District
(%) (N = 2,993)

Landholding Status	Dinajpur	Gaibandha	Kurigram	Lalmonirhat	Rangpur	All Districts
Landless (<0.5 acre)	67.2	82.8	83.2	75.7	83.4	78.2
Marginal holders (>=0.5 acre and <1 acre)	12.3	9.6	7.5	9.8	7.2	9.4
Small holders (>=1 acre and <2.5 acres)	16.0	7.0	8.1	11.3	7.2	10.0
Medium holders (>=2.5 acre and <7.5 acres)	4.6	0.6	0.7	2.7	2.2	2.2
Large holders (>7.5 acres)	0.0	0.0	0.6	0.5	0.0	0.2

Source: Authors' calculations based on the ADB–BIDS Digital Microcredit Survey 2021.

Table 4 shows that on average, 42.5% of household heads of the sample households have no education at all. This percentage is the highest in Lalmonirhat (43.4%) and the lowest in Kurigram (37.7%). About 56% of household heads have at least some education below the primary level. The numbers for primary, secondary, and higher secondary education and above are 12.1%, 7.5%, and 7.6%, respectively. Households in Kurigram district have the highest percentage (12.6%) of household heads with higher secondary education and above. The lowest share is in Dinajpur (5.3%).

Table 4: Distribution of Households by Household Head's Education
(%) (N = 2,993)

Head's Education	Dinajpur	Gaibandha	Kurigram	Lalmonirhat	Rangpur	All Districts
None	49.0	48.0	37.7	49.4	43.4	42.5
Below primary	60.0	55.4	59.0	49.3	57.4	56.0
Primary	10.7	13.4	10.0	14.7	11.3	12.1
Secondary	6.9	7.9	8.4	6.6	7.9	7.5
Higher secondary and above	5.3	5.7	12.6	8.4	6.9	7.6

Source: Authors' calculations based on the ADB–BIDS Digital Microcredit Survey 2021.

Table 5 presents the proportion of households earning income from different occupations. The occupation categories are not mutually exclusive, and a household can earn from multiple sources. Of the sample households, 26.6% earn from farm occupation. The highest proportion of farm occupation is in Kurigram (33.3%) and the lowest is in Gaibandha (21.9%). On average, the proportion of households earning income from a wage occupation is 39.8%, with the highest percentage in Kurigram (57.8%) and the lowest in Dinajpur (20.7%). The percentage of households who earn from farm self-employment is the highest in Lalmonirhat (48.3%) and the lowest in Rangpur (34.9%), with an average of 42.4% in all five districts. MSME business contributes to the earnings of 13.3% households, on average, whereas the numbers for MSME services and MSME manufacturing are 10.4% and 9.0%, respectively.

Table 5: Distribution of Households by Occupational Status
(%) (N = 2,993)

Household's Main Occupation	Dinajpur	Gaibandha	Kurigram	Lalmonirhat	Rangpur	All Districts
Farm wage	27.5	21.9	33.3	28.0	24.0	26.6
Nonfarm wage	20.7	48.2	57.8	35.4	41.0	39.8
Farm self	44.3	39.9	45.2	48.3	34.9	42.4
MSME business	11.8	9.6	20.6	14.9	11.1	13.3
MSME service	7.3	6.8	19.8	13.5	6.4	10.4
MSME manufacturing	3.5	7.3	19.7	11.5	5.2	9.0
Other	0.9	2.3	11.6	5.6	1.1	4.0

MSME = micro, small, and medium-sized enterprise.

Source: Authors' calculations based on the ADB–BIDS Digital Microcredit Survey 2021.

Table 6 shows that almost all (97.7%) households of the sample have at least one mobile phone. However, the ownership of a smartphone is much lower, only 36.6% on average. The percentage of households using a mobile phone to access the internet is 32.3%, with the highest and lowest proportions in Kurigram (38.1%) and Rangpur (26.2%), respectively. On average, 19.7% of households use mobile phones for business purposes.

Table 6: Distribution of Households by Mobile Phone Ownership and Use
(%) (N = 2,993)

Mobile Phone Variables	Dinajpur	Gaibandha	Kurigram	Lalmonirhat	Rangpur	All Districts
Household has mobile phones	98.6	97.6	98.9	95.6	98.1	97.7
Household has smartphones	41.9	33.6	37.4	35.3	34.8	36.6
Household uses mobile phones to access internet	37.9	28.9	38.1	31.5	26.2	32.3
Household uses mobile phones for business purposes	21.3	23.3	26.7	13.3	15.4	19.7

Source: Authors' calculations based on the ADB–BIDS Digital Microcredit Survey 2021.

Table 7 reveals that more than 90% of villages in all five districts have access to grid electricity; however, in Lalmonirhat it is much lower compared with the other four districts with only 62.0% of this district having grid access. Also in Lalmonirhat, 96.2% (the highest among all five districts) of rural roads are paved, whereas the percentage for Dinajpur is only 64.0% (the lowest among all five districts). Of all sample villages, 91.0% have primary schools. The percentage for secondary school is 44.3%.

On average, 63.9% of villages have at least one market. Slightly more than half of the villages (54.1%) in the sample have at least one health center, with the highest percentage in Lalmonirhat (69.2% of villages) and the lowest in Dinajpur (28.0% of villages)

Table 7: Share of Villages with Selected Physical Infrastructures
(%) (N = 122)

Village	Dinajpur	Gaibandha	Kurigram	Lalmonirhat	Rangpur	All Districts
Share of households in village with grid electricity	99.8	97.2	94.3	62.0	99.1	90.1
Paved roads	64.0	69.2	65.0	96.2	84.0	76.2
Primary schools	92.0	92.3	90.0	92.3	88.0	91.0
Secondary schools	32.0	38.5	40.0	57.7	52.0	44.3
Markets	52.0	57.7	60.0	84.6	64.0	63.9
Health centers	28.0	57.7	65.0	69.2	52.0	54.1

Source: Authors' calculations based on the ADB–BIDS Digital Microcredit Survey 2021.

We see from **Table 8** that less than 10% of villages have a branch of commercial bank. However, the presence of microcredit programs is higher: 18% for all districts, 35% (the highest) for Kurigram, and 7.7% (the lowest) for Gaibandha. There is at least one MFS agent in three out of four villages in the sample. The percentage of villages with any financial services is 77% on average.

Table 8: Share of Villages with Selected Financial Infrastructures and Services
(%) (N = 122)

Village Infrastructures/ Services	Dinajpur	Gaibandha	Kurigram	Lalmonirhat	Rangpur	All Districts
Commercial bank branches	8.0	7.7	15.0	11.5	8.0	9.8
Microcredit programs	16.0	7.7	35.0	15.4	20.0	18.0
MFS agents	64.0	69.2	75.0	76.9	92.0	75.4
Any financial services	68.0	73.1	75.0	76.9	92.0	77.0

MFS = mobile financial services.

Source: Authors' calculations based on the ADB–BIDS Digital Microcredit Survey 2021.

The average village-level agricultural wage for male workers is Tk376 per day, with little deviation from the mean across districts (**Table 9**). The female wage rate is much lower in all districts at only Tk234 per day on average. The highest and lowest female wage rates are in Dinajpur (Tk264 per day) and Lalmonirhat (Tk198 per day), respectively.

Table 9: Village-Level Agricultural Wages of Men and Women
(N = 122)

Agricultural Wage	Dinajpur	Gaibandha	Kurigram	Lalmonirhat	Rangpur	All Districts
Male wage (Tk/day)	386.0	378.9	368.0	359.6	390.0	376.7
Female wage (Tk/day)	264.2	241.5	210.3	198.1	256.8	234.9
Ratio of female–male	0.68	0.64	0.57	0.55	0.66	0.62

Sources: Village census and household surveys.

Discussion

Among the census population surveyed in the five districts, in terms of microfinance participation, ASA members are observed to be the largest group on average, both in terms of participants who are member of ASA and at least one other MFI as well from those who are members of only ASA. This is seen from the household sample as well. Landless households (those with less than 0.5 acres of land) appear to be over 78% of total households in all districts, the highest being in Gaibandha, Kurigram, and Rangpur. Shares of marginal and small landholders are roughly the same in all districts overall (9.4% and 10.0%). The majority of household members are self-employed in farming or agricultural work, followed by wage employment. A total of 13.3% of all households are involved in MSME business activities, 10.4% are involved in service activities, and 9.0% are in MSME manufacturing activities. While MFS agents have relatively high penetration in all villages, digitalized microcredit programs are still very low in all villages. Although mobile phone ownership is almost 98%, smartphone ownership and internet use are much lower, and use of mobiles for business purposes is even lower. If digital financial services are adopted by MFIs, comfort with smartphone usage will also have to increase simultaneously among village members.

3. Defining MSMEs and Their Relevance to Meeting the Sustainable Development Goals

MSMEs are defined somewhat differently by different agencies, according to existing literature. Over time, there have been multiple definitions often causing confusion when comparing various data with respect to MSME (**Table 10**). Bangladesh's National Industrial Policy, 2010, while defining the size of enterprises from micro to small and large, uses two criteria: the number of workers employed in the enterprise and the value of fixed assets (excluding land and building). The definition also uses different thresholds in these criteria for manufacturing and service enterprises. For manufacturing and service firms, microenterprises are those with either the value of fixed assets of Tk0.5 million to Tk5 million or between 10 and 24 workers. For manufacturing firms, small enterprises either have a value of fixed assets between Tk5 million and Tk100 million or between 25 and 99 workers. Medium-sized enterprises are defined as firms with either a value of fixed assets between Tk100 million and Tk300 million or between 100 and 250 workers. For service firms, small enterprises should either have a fixed asset value from Tk0.5 million to Tk10 million or between 10 and 25 employees. Medium-sized enterprises, according to the updated 2016 industrial policy, are those with fixed asset valued between Tk10 million and Tk150 million or between 50 and 100 workers. In all cases, if a firm falls into a large category according to one criterion and small category according to the other, the firm will be defined as being large. The updated MSME definition adopted in the 2016 industrial policy is broadly accepted at the policy level.

Table 10: Definitions of MSME in Bangladesh

Type	Sector	Fixed Assets Other Than Land and Buildings (Tk million)				Number of Employees			
		2003	2010	2016	2016-new	2003	2010	2016	2016-new
Cottage		–	–	< 1	–	–	–	<= 15	–
Micro	Manufacturing	–	0.5–5	1–7.5	0.5–5	0–9	10–24	16–30	10–24
	Business				< 0.5				< 10
	Service		<= 0.5		< 0.5		<= 10		< 5
Small	Manufacturing	–	5–100	7.5–150	5–100	10–49	25–99	31–120	25–99
	Business				0.5–10				6–10
	Service		0.5–10	1–20	0.5–10		10–25	16–50	10–49
Medium	Manufacturing	–	100–300	150–500	100–300	50–99	100–250	121–300	100–150
	Business				10–150				11–50
	Service		0.5–10	20–300	10–150		50–100	51–120	50–100
Large		–	–	–	–	>= 100	–	–	–

MSME = micro, small, and medium-sized enterprise.

Sources: Economic Census 2003, Bangladesh Bureau of Statistics; Doing Business 2018, International Finance Corporation; National Industrial Policy, Government of Bangladesh, 2016 (cited in Andrianaivo et al. 2019); Credit and Development Forum, 2016 (cited in Andrianaivo et al. 2019).

The Economic Census 2013 provides distribution of MSMEs by major economic activities (**Table 11**). For micro and small enterprises, the majority of activities are in trading (44% and 62%, respectively), followed by other services (25.5% and 29%, respectively), whereas for medium-sized enterprises most activities are split equally between manufacturing and other services (42% for both). Other industrial activities comprise the smallest share for micro and small enterprises (0.4% and 0.9%, respectively), while transport and storage comprise the smallest share for medium-sized firms (2.3%). Micro and small firms largely differ from each other in manufacturing and in transport and storage: For both of these activities, micro firms have much higher involvement than small firms (12.0% as opposed to 3.6% in manufacturing, and 18.2% as opposed to 4.4% in trading and storage).

Table 11: Distribution of Enterprises by Major Economic Activity, 2013
(`000)

Sector	Micro		Small		Medium		Large		All	
	Number	%	Number	%	Number	%	Number	%	Number	%
Manufacturing	831.2	12.0	30.9	3.6	3.0	42.1	3.12	59.4	868.2	11.1
Other industrial activities	26.1	0.4	7.8	0.9	0.3	4.6	0.17	3.2	34.3	0.4
Trading and related activities	3,057.7	44.0	531.0	61.8	0.6	8.9	0.08	1.5	3,589.5	45.9
Transport and storage	1,265.9	18.2	37.7	4.4	0.2	2.3	0.04	0.8	1,303.8	16.7
Other services	1,766.0	25.4	251.9	29.3	3.0	42.2	1.84	35.0	2,022.7	25.9
Total	6,946.9	100.0	859.3	100.0	7.1	100.0	5.25	100.0	7,818.6	100.0

Source: Bangladesh Bureau of Statistics. 2013. *Economic Census*. Dhaka.

The cottage, micro, small, and medium-sized enterprises (CMSMEs) have the greatest potential in creating employment and income generation in rural as well as urban areas. As reported in the government's Eighth Five-Year Plan, these enterprises account for over 99% of all enterprises and about 83% of employment. The lack of dynamism and informal global evidence suggests that CMSMEs contribute to growth through employment and export promotion. As observed, the young unemployed population could benefit from the promotion of CMSME jobs. Hence, CMSME financing and growth could effectively promote several Sustainable Development Goal (SDG) targets. Necessarily, the Eighth Five-Year Plan of the Government of Bangladesh places strong emphasis on dynamism, removing the institutional constraints they face and improving their financing options through collaboration between SME foundations and the central bank, Bangladesh Bank.

Expansion of microcredit in financing CMSMEs could play a vital role in poverty reduction as in the past. Information and communication technology-based financial products and instruments such as mobile banking could revolutionize the financial access and services to the poor in rural and urban areas. The installation of the Microcredit Regulatory Authority in 2010 brought forth a regulatory framework to protect lenders and borrowers. During the 2015–2019 period, the number of borrowers increased by over 5 million and loan amounts doubled from Tk634 billion to Tk1,335 billion.

Different Types of MSME: What Does Recent Economic Census Say?

According to the latest Economic Census in 2013, the numbers of micro, small, and medium-sized establishments in Bangladesh are, respectively, 104,007; 859,318; and 7,106. The combined figure is 970,431 for the whole

MSME sector. Permanent establishments in the "wholesale and retail trade, repair of motor vehicles and motorcycles" category accounts for 56.2% of total permanent establishments in the country (**Table 12**). "Accommodation and food service activities," manufacturing," and "education' represent 9.4%, 8.7%, and 4.2%, respectively.

All (100%) of the country's permanent microenterprises are manufacturing firms (**Table 12**). Among permanent small enterprises, 62.8% fall into the "wholesale and retail trade, repair of motor vehicles and motorcycles" category, while "education" and "manufacturing" account for 9.6% and 3.9%, respectively, of the small permanent establishments. Medium-sized permanent establishments are often manufacturing firms (41.8%). The second- and third-largest activities among medium-sized permanent establishments are "education" and "public administration."

Table 12: Distribution of Type of Firm According to the Economic Census

Sector	Type					Total
	Cottage	Micro	Small	Medium	Large	
Mining and quarrying	12,744	0	1,075	41	19	13,879
	0.34	0	0.14	0.57	0.36	0.3
Manufacturing	284,499	81,521	30,967	3,006	3,141	403,134
	7.63	100	3.91	41.77	59.31	8.74
Electricity, gas, steam, and air conditioning supply	1,915	0	1,502	136	84	3,637
	0.05	0	0.19	1.89	1.59	0.08
Water supply, sewerage, waste management, and remediation activities	1,469	0	538	18	13	2,038
	0.04	0	0.07	0.25	0.25	0.04
Construction	654	0	4,063	139	57	4,913
	0.02	0	0.51	1.93	1.08	0.11
Wholesale and retail trade, repair of motor vehicles and motorcycles	2,096,192	0	496,691	630	79	2,593,592
	56.22	0	62.75	8.75	1.49	56.21
Transportation and storage	48,553	0	13,935	158	39	62,685
	1.3	0	1.76	2.2	0.74	1.36
Accommodation and food service activities (hotel and restaurants)	418,337	0	16,781	59	23	435,200
	11.22	0	2.12	0.82	0.43	9.43
Information and communication	7,834	0	10,753	58	44	18,689
	0.21	0	1.36	0.81	0.83	0.41
Financial and insurance activities	18,591	0	28,322	398	489	47,800
	0.5	0	3.58	5.53	9.23	1.04
Real estate activities	224	0	4,789	41	21	5,075
	0.01	0	0.61	0.57	0.4	0.11
Professional, scientific, and technical activities	30,686	0	8,734	103	73	39,596
	0.82	0	1.1	1.43	1.38	0.86
Administrative and support service activities	33,233	0	10,912	52	21	44,218
	0.89	0	1.38	0.72	0.4	0.96
Public administration	15,807	0	9,527	794	680	26,808
	0.42	0	1.2	11.03	12.84	0.58
Education	114,965	0	75,623	980	181	191,749
	3.08	0	9.55	13.62	3.42	4.16

continued on next page

Table 12 continued

Sector	Type					Total
	Cottage	Micro	Small	Medium	Large	
Human health and social work activities	53,384	0	17,774	492	312	71,962
	1.43	0	2.25	6.84	5.89	1.56
Art, entertainment, and recreation	8,193	0	1,672	19	3	9,887
	0.22	0	0.21	0.26	0.06	0.21
Other service activities	581,062	0	57,827	73	17	638,979
	15.58	0	7.31	1.01	0.32	13.85
Total	3,728,342	81,521	791,485	7,197	5,296	4,613,841
	100	100	100	100	100	100

Notes: Upper = number, lower = percentage share.

Source: Bangladesh Bureau of Statistics. 2013. *Economic Census*. Dhaka.

Among the five sample districts of our study, Rangpur and Kurigram, respectively, have the highest (37,546) and lowest (2,986) number of MSME establishments (**Table 13**). In Lalmonirhat, more than 80% of the MSME establishments are categorized as small.

Table 13: Distribution of MSMEs in Surveyed Districts According to the Economic Census

District	Micro Industry	Small Industry	Medium Industry	Large Industry	No. Total Establishments	Total MSMEs
Dinajpur	0.5	2.4	0	2.9	2,16,115	6,267.3
Gaibandha	0.4	2.1	0	2.5	1,51,052	3,776.3
Kurigram	0.3	2.1	0	2.4	1,24,450	2,986.8
Lalmonirhat	9.5	39	0	48.5	72,075	34,956.4
Rangpur	1.9	18.5	0.1	20.5	1,83,153	37,546.4

Source: Bangladesh Bureau of Statistics. 2013. *Economic Census*. Dhaka.

Table 14 shows that 2.4% and 0.5% of establishments in Dinajpur are small and microenterprises, respectively, with no medium-sized enterprises. A similar distribution is seen in Gaibandha and Kurigram, according to the Economic Census 2013. The average size of MSME firms is larger in Lalmonirhat and Rangpur. Of all the establishments in Lalmonirhat, 39.0% are small and 9.5% are micro. In Rangpur, the respective percentages are 18.5% and 1.9%.

Table 14: District-Wise Share of Types of Establishments of Rangpur Division
(%)

District	Cottage Industry	Micro Industry	Small Industry	Medium Industry	Large Industry	No. Total Establishments
Dinajpur	97.0	0.5	2.4	0.0	0.0	216,115
Gaibandha	97.4	0.4	2.1	0.0	0.0	151,052
Kurigram	97.6	0.3	2.1	0.0	0.0	124,450
Lalmonirhat	51.5	9.5	39.0	0.0	0.0	72,075
Rangpur	79.5	1.9	18.5	0.1	0.0	183,153

Source: Bangladesh Bureau of Statistics. *Economic Census*. 2013.

Policies Shaping MSME Expansion and Financing

Because of the multisector focus of MSMEs, financing and expansion policies and their implementation involves several institutional bodies, including the Ministry of Industry, the Ministry of Finance, the Ministry of Commerce, Bangladesh Bank, SME Foundation, the Bangladesh Small and Cottage Industries Corporation (BSCIC), the Bangladesh Council of Scientific and Industrial Research, the Bangladesh Industrial Technical Assistance Centre, and the Business Promotion Council (Andrianaivo et al. 2019).[2] The Ministry of Industry recently assumed a central role in industrial policy among the interministerial agencies. The Bank for Small Industries and Commerce was created to support financing of small industries in 1988. Bangladesh Bank assumes the regulatory and financing roles for the sector. While the central role in terms of policy-setting is played by the Ministry of Industry, Bangladesh Bank regulates issues related to the financing of the MSME sector through national financial institutions, including banks and nonbank finance institutions (NBFIs). Bangladesh Bank undertakes initiatives for the development of MSMEs, with a particular focus on women entrepreneurs. Bangladesh Bank adopted MSME credit policies in 2011, while formally distinguishing MSMEs and prioritizing MSME activities with special emphasis on women entrepreneurs and MSME lending by commercial banks, simplifying the rules and procedures for small-enterprise lending, as well as the relaxation of collateral requirements. More importantly, a special department was created in the Bangladesh Bank to stimulate the MSME activities, and monitoring and development of the sector.

Among the regulatory policies of Bangladesh Bank for MSMEs, the primary ones cover loan provisioning, capital allocation, a cluster approach to financing, credit rating, and loan size. For example, Bangladesh Bank's loan-provisioning options for MSME financing allows only 0.25% for general provisioning as opposed to other financing such as housing and consumer loans. Capital is charged against risk-weighted assets for MSME loans as follows: a loan of less than Tk3 million MSME with unrated assets receives a 75% risk weight and for a loan amount greater the risk weight is 100%.

Bangladesh Bank sets a yearly goal of MSME loan disbursement for each financial institution and closely monitors their progress. There are area-wise targets of MSME loan disbursement that the banks and NBFIs have to achieve. The banks and NBFIs are allowed to follow a separate business strategy for the MSME loans that ease the administrative formalities and facilitates the disbursement of loans within the shortest possible time.

Based on Bangladesh Bank directives, banks and NBFIs give special attention to MSME clusters in terms of financing. The banks and NBFIs have been instructed that at least 30% of total loans should go to the MSMEs. Women entrepreneurs are given priority and special attention in terms of MSME loans from banks and MSMEs.

Bangladesh Bank provides refinancing schemes for SME lending through its own funds as well as using donor finance. The latter includes multilateral and other bilateral donor partners such as the Asian Development Bank (ADB) and the Japan International Cooperation Agency (JICA). Through the refinancing scheme, Bangladesh Bank supports low-cost funds to MSMEs through its partner financial institutions mandated to offer prescribed maximum interest rates to be charged to specific borrowers such as women entrepreneurs.

Institutional Financing Patterns of MSMEs

Evidence suggests MSMEs have access to various sources of finance including their own sources of capital. In the case of new entrepreneurs, own-finance serves as the major source, dependence on which decreases over time as the enterprise grows. MSMEs are financed through various institutional mechanisms including nongovernment

---

[2]   The following policy related discussion draws on the review of Andrianaivo et al. (2019).

organizations (NGOs) and microcredit and credit facilities from the banking sector. Access to bank finance increases with the size of the enterprise. It is found that the intensity of bank credit is less than 4% for microenterprises as opposed to 25% for medium-sized enterprises (Khalily and Khaleque 2018). Khalily and Khaleque (2018) analyzed the credit constraints and productivity issues of household enterprises using nationally representative 2010 survey data and found that many enterprises are credit-constrained despite having some form of financing through NGOs and microcredit lenders. Earlier evidence suggests that MSMEs have limited access to bank loans due to high transaction costs and collateral issues, among others.

Loans through microcredit institution are a major source of finance for MSMEs in Bangladesh. The major NGOs (BRAC and ASA), GB, as well as Palli Karma Sahayak Foundation (PKSF) partner organizations are all active in providing loan to microenterprises and entrepreneurs. The Microcredit Regulatory Authority (MRA) is the regulating body of the government that oversee the MFI activities. The operation of these MFIs is based on group guarantees from the borrowers rather than individual collateral. As of 2016, the MFIs have 37.7 million members. The size of an average loan distributed by the MFIs is around Tk30,000.

MSME credit from the formal banking sector has seen high growth in recent years; the growth was 18% per annum from 2010 to 2016. Most of the MSME loans go to trading activities (around 60%), whereas the percentage going to service and manufacturing MSMEs are around 10% and 30%, respectively. MSME loans account for 23.9% of total loans outstanding from the bank and nonbank sector in Bangladesh. The public commercial banks and private commercial banks give 18.4% and 27.1%, respectively, of their total loans to MSMEs, while 11.4% of total loans from NBFIs are distributed to the MSMEs.

The MFIs supply the most loans to microenterprises. In 2016, 86.8% of total loans to microenterprises came from the MFIs. The rest came from banks (11.1%) and other public institutions (2.1%). In 2016, the total loan amount to microenterprises amounted to Tk1,030 billion.

The COVID-19 pandemic has undoubtedly increased the demand for loans for MSMEs. According to Bangladesh Bank statistics, the Government of Bangladesh announced a stimulus package targeting MSMEs in April 2020. The 3-year initial plan is supposed to distribute Tk200 billion at a 4% interest rate through the formal banking channel. As of September 2020, 21,000 entrepreneurs were approved for total lending of Tk55,000 million from that stimulus package and Tk37,000 million had been distributed.

Role of Finance in Relation to Nonfinancial Constraints

The financing challenges for MSME are discussed in both academic and policy papers. Generally, both demand- and supply-side factors can constrain MSMEs development and growth. The lack of financial capabilities and informality are often cited as demand-side constraints; however, high financing costs also act as demand deterrence factor. The supply-side constraint factors include financial institutions' risk aversion in MSME lending resulting from inadequate credit appraisal policies, credit infrastructure, and risk management tools. It is also observed that MSMEs become further credit-constrained resulting from the crowding out of commercial bank financing by public sector organizations (Andrianaivo et al. 2019).

Among the financing constraints, the poor quality of collateral, documentation, and business plans are cited. MSMEs are often considered high-risk borrowers because of a lack of assets and capitalization. The major obstacle cited as MSME financing the "bank's reliance on collateral-based lending." The commercial banks often repackage their existing products as MSME products and are often criticized for only responding to government credit guarantee facilities in providing loan to MSMEs. However, commercial banks also offer innovative financing for MSMEs.

According to the 2013 Enterprise Survey of the World Bank, smaller firms face higher collateral requirements relative to the value of loans, compared with medium-sized and large firms.

Characteristics of Microenterprises Surveyed

A sample of 2,993 households out of a population of 24,701 were surveyed in five districts: Dinajpur, Gaibandha, Kurigram, Lalmonirhat, and Rangpur. According to census data, 15.4% of the firms are businesses, 0.4% are manufacturing, and 8.7% are services and others (**Table 15**). The remaining 75.5% are non-MSME households.

Table 15: Census Distribution of Household-Owned and -Operated Nonfarm Enterprise (%) (N = 24,701)

Categories of Nonfarm Activities	Freq.	Percent
Business	3,810	15.42
Manufacturing	99	0.4
Service and others	2,153	8.72
None	18,639	75.46
Total	24,701	100

Source: Authors' calculations based on the ADB–BIDS Digital Microcredit Survey 2021.

The district-wise distribution of nonfarm activities is shown in **Table 16**. Within Dinajpur, 13.1% of the firms surveyed are businesses, while the percentage for manufacturing and services are 0.2% and 8.7%, respectively. In Kurigram, 23.3% of the sample firms are businesses, 10.1% are services, and 0.5% are manufacturing.

Table 16: District-Wise Census Distribution of Household-Owned and -Operated Nonfarm Enterprise (%) (N = 24,701)

Nonfarm Activities	Dinajpur	Gaibandha	Kurigram	Lalmonirhat	Rangpur	Total
Business	13.13	13.8	23.3	14.93	13.56	15.42
Manufacturing	0.19	0.38	0.46	0.58	0.4	0.4
Service and others	8.73	10.78	10.14	5.5	8.77	8.72
None	77.95	75.04	66.1	78.99	77.27	75.46

Source: Authors' calculations based on the ADB–BIDS Digital Microcredit Survey 2021.

Distribution of Microenterprises by Major Sectors

The Economic Census 2013 categorizes the industrial establishments into three mutually exclusive categories: household-based, permanent, and temporary. In the five sample districts, 48.1% of the establishments are household-based, while the percentages for permanent and temporary establishments are 47.6% and 4.3%, respectively (**Table 17**). The distribution is similar within each individual districts.

Table 17: District-Wise Distribution of Type of Establishments
(%)

Establishments	Dinajpur	Gaibandha	Kurigram	Lalmonirhat	Rangpur	Total
Household	49.79	50.96	50.26	43.88	43.73	48.05
Permanent Establishments	47.74	44.82	45.52	53.12	49.06	47.62
Temporary Establishments	2.47	4.22	4.21	3	7.21	4.33

Source: Bangladesh Bureau of Statistics. 2013. *Economic Census*. Dhaka.

Table 18 shows the distribution of industrial establishments in the five sample districts by type of economic activities. In 2013, the highest proportion of establishments fell in the "wholesale and retail trade, repair of motor vehicles and motorcycles" category (43.65%). The second-largest proportion (27.4%) was in "transportation and storage" category. Manufacturing establishments accounted for 7.3% of the total establishments. Some other categories are "accommodation and food service activities" (3.8%), "education" (2.4%), and "human health and social work activities" (1.2%). The distributions in the individual districts are similar as in the average distribution.

Table 18: District-Wise Distribution of MSME Establishments by Sector
(%)

Sector	Dinajpur	Gaibandha	Kurigram	Lalmonirhat	Rangpur	Total
Mining and quarrying	0	0	0.02	0.03	0.01	0.01
Manufacturing	6.38	6.84	8.57	12.44	6.01	7.33
Electricity, gas, steam, and air conditioning supply	0.03	0.02	0.04	0.03	0.04	0.03
Water supply, sewerage, waste management, and remediation activities	0.06	0.01	0.19	0.02	0.01	0.05
Construction	0.12	0.05	0.04	0.04	0.23	0.11
Wholesale and retail trade, repair of motor vehicles and motorcycles	43.1	41.51	47.8	44.67	42.85	43.65
Transportation and storage	26.95	32.52	22.1	23.16	29.03	27.41
Accommodation and food service activities (hotel and restaurants)	3.71	3.61	3.57	3.99	4.24	3.82
Information and communication	0.13	0.12	0.23	0.17	0.24	0.17
Financial and insurance activities	0.52	0.46	0.41	0.51	0.63	0.51
Real estate activities	0.05	0	0	0.01	0.02	0.02
Professional, scientific, and technical activities	0.46	0.41	0.52	0.57	0.4	0.46
Administrative and support service activities	0.55	0.35	0.34	0.38	0.38	0.42
Public administration	0.35	0.19	0.32	0.36	0.27	0.29
Education	2.34	2.37	2.46	2.79	2.24	2.39

continued on next page

Table 18 continued

Sector	Dinajpur	Gaibandha	Kurigram	Lalmonirhat	Rangpur	Total
Human health and social work activities	1.47	1.09	1.01	1.22	1.16	1.22
Art, entertainment, and recreation	0.09	0.06	0.08	0.05	0.07	0.07
Other service activities	13.69	10.38	12.31	9.56	12.18	12.02

MSME = micro, small, and medium-sized enterprise.

Source: Bangladesh Bureau of Statistics. 2013. *Economic Census*. Dhaka.

Discussion

While there is variation of definitions of MSMEs used over time, we now have agreed-upon criteria thanks to policy recognition of MSMEs' importance in the economy. The 2013 Economic Census revealed that for micro and small firms, the majority of activities are in trading, followed by other services. For medium-sized firms, activities are mostly divided between manufacturing and other services. Cottage, micro, and small enterprises hold the highest potential for employment and income generation in both rural and urban areas and promoting these enterprises can greatly expand employment and help meet multiple SDG targets. Generally, both demand- and supply-side factors can constrain MSMEs development and growth. The lack of financial capabilities and informality are often cited as demand-side constraints, while the supply-side constraint factors include financial institutions' risk aversion in MSME lending, resulting from inadequate credit appraisal policies, credit infrastructure, and risk management tools. The Government of Bangladesh's long-term development policies envision development of MSMEs and their financial access. Under the leadership of Bangladesh Bank, an extension of the microcredit facility has been emphasized since 2011.

4. State of Microfinance and Microfinance Institutions

Clientele Outreach and Loan Disbursement

In Bangladesh, MFI membership grew from almost 35 million in 2010 to more than 41 million by 2020. **Figure 1** shows that membership grew steadily from 2013 to 2020. Starting in 2008, membership declined due to the slow growth of non-GB MFI membership (Khandker et al. 2016). The annual growth of microfinance membership and active borrowers are reported in **Table 19**. This growth shows a positive trend from 2013. Table 19 also shows the annual growth in outstanding borrowers of the MFIs. Like membership growth, the growth in outstanding borrowers was negative in 2012 and 2013, and was positive again from 2014 to 2019.

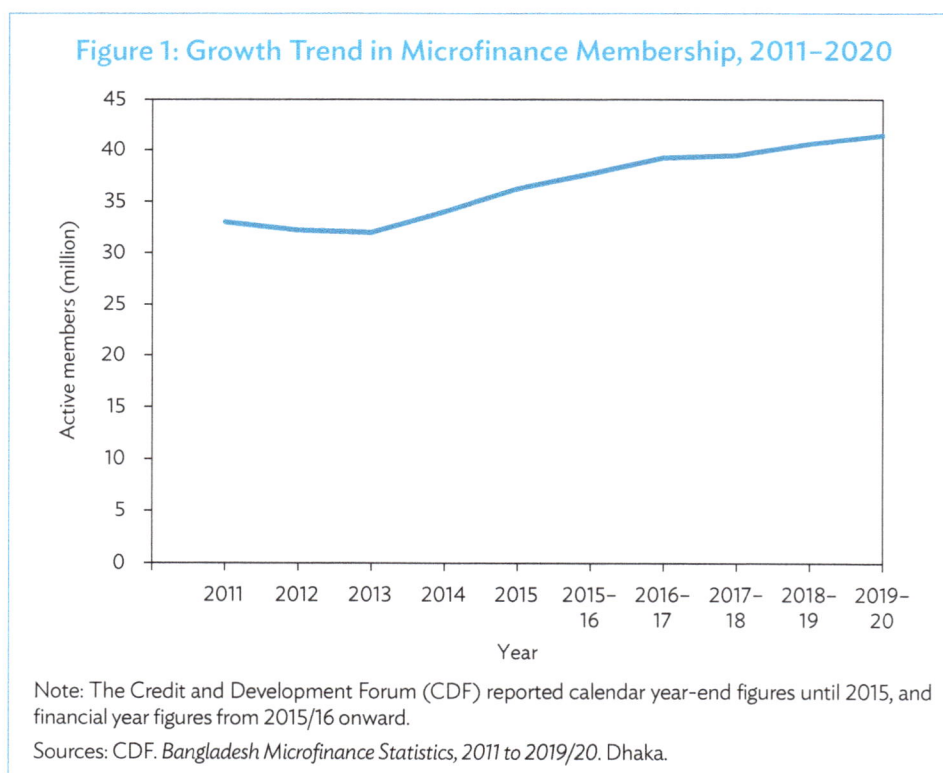

Figure 1: Growth Trend in Microfinance Membership, 2011–2020

Note: The Credit and Development Forum (CDF) reported calendar year-end figures until 2015, and financial year figures from 2015/16 onward.

Sources: CDF. *Bangladesh Microfinance Statistics, 2011 to 2019/20*. Dhaka.

However, during the same period, MFI loan disbursements increased steadily from 2011 to 2018–2019 (**Figure 2**). The amount disbursed was slightly more than Tk440 billion in 2011, growing to about Tk1,426 billion by 2019/20.

Table 19: Annual Growth in Microfinance Clientele in Bangladesh, 2011–2020
(%)

Year	Active Members	Outstanding Borrowers
2011	−5.52	0.33
2012	−2.47	−4.49
2013	−0.73	−1.08
2014	6.34	6.11
2015	6.44	8.63
2015/16	3.93	3.43
2016/17	4.14	6.01
2017/18	0.65	−2.98
2018/19	2.90	2.97
2019/20	2.08	−0.22

Note: The Credit and Development Forum (CDF) reported calendar year-end figures until 2015, and financial year figures from 2015/16 onward.

Sources: CDF. *Bangladesh Microfinance Statistics, 2011 to 2019/20*. Dhaka.

Figure 2: Microfinance Institution Loan Disbursement Trend in Bangladesh, 2011–2020

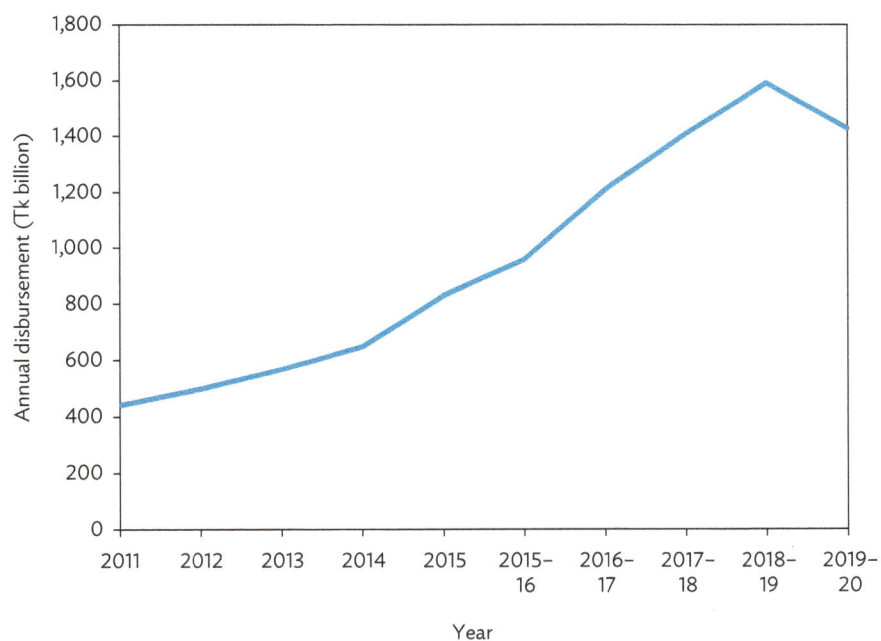

Note: The Credit and Development Forum (CDF) reported calendar year-end figures until 2015, and financial year figures from 2015/16 onward.

Sources: CDF. *Bangladesh Microfinance Statistics, 2011 to 2019/20*. Dhaka.

How Much Savings Was Mobilized?

Savings for the MFIs was a little over Tk185 billion in 2011, increasing steadily to over Tk542 billion by 2019/20 (**Figure 3**), with a drop to about Tk158 billion in 2012. Similar to the trend in the previous decade, the trend in savings as a percentage of loans outstanding somewhat fluctuated from 2011 to 2020. It dropped from 66% in 2011 to over 50% in 2012, before rising to over 55% in 2014, and then falling again to almost 45% in 2016/17 (**Figure 4**). It climbed again to 52% in 2019/20. Since cumulative savings increased steadily since 2012, the opposite pattern observed in Figure 4 is due entirely to the volume of loans outstanding.

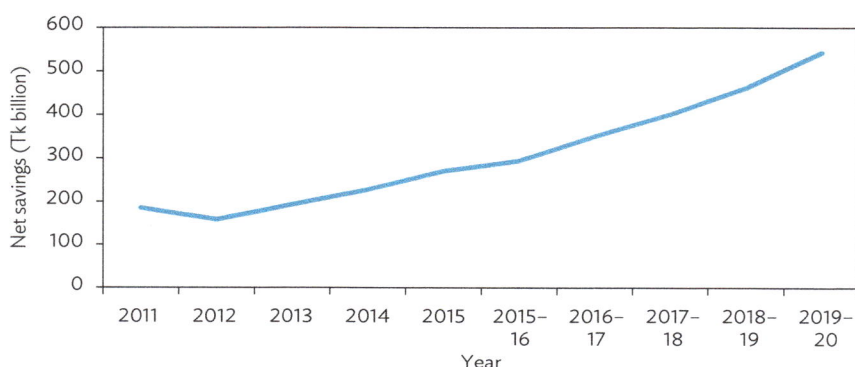

Figure 3: Savings Mobilized by Microfinance Institutions in Bangladesh, 2011–2020

Note: The Credit and Development Forum (CDF) reported calendar year-end figures until 2015, and financial year figures from 2015/16 onward.

Sources: CDF. *Bangladesh Microfinance Statistics, 2011 to 2019/20*. Dhaka.

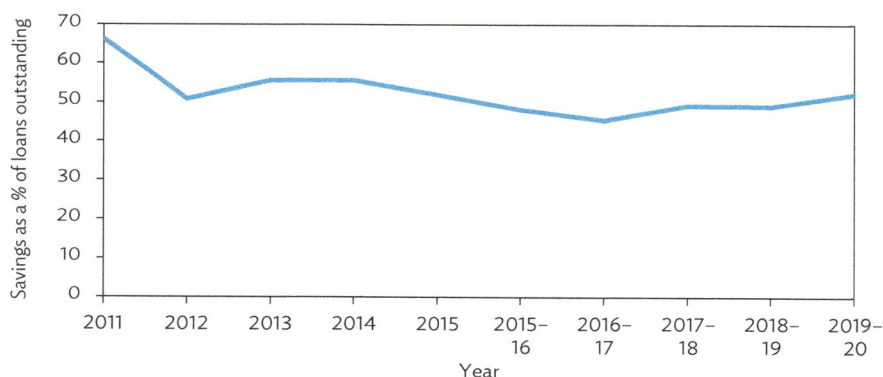

Figure 4: Savings as a Share of Microfinance Institution Loans Outstanding in Bangladesh, 2011–2020

Note: The Credit and Development Forum (CDF) reported calendar year-end figures until 2015, and financial year figures from 2015/16 onward.

Sources: CDF. *Bangladesh Microfinance Statistics, 2011 to 2019/20*. Dhaka.

Sector Composition of Microfinance Institution Lending

Table 20 compares the sector-wise distribution of MFI loans from 2011 to 2019/20. Agriculture-related activities had the highest share throughout. Agriculture comprises various activities including crop production, fisheries, and livestock and poultry.

Table 20: Comparison of Sector-Wise Distribution of Microfinance Disbursement (%)

Sector	Year									
	2011	2012	2013	2014	2015	2015/16	2016/17	2017/18	2018/19	2019/20
Agriculture	46.79	46.04	47.08	47.17	46.99	49.98	49.35	43.92	45.67	49.86
Trade and business	39.78	22.86	29.06	28.91	46.22	30.91	34.08	21.81	27.60	26.68
Small and cottage industries	3.09	2.65	1.92	1.69	1.56	1.97	2.29	13.72	3.58	3.33
Social sector	7.61	6.93	2.29	1.66	1.74	2.84	2.59	2.41	0.92	0.81
Transport and communication	2.73	2.08	3.30	3.03	3.48	3.72	4.07	6.98	3.82	4.11
Others	–	19.44	16.35	17.53	–	10.58	7.61	11.16	18.41	15.20

Notes: The Credit and Development Forum (CDF) reported calendar year-end figures until 2015, and financial year figures from 2015/16 onward. Agriculture includes crops, nursery, water irrigation, livestock, dairy, poultry, fish, and cultivation. Social sector includes health and medication, education, and infrastructure. Other includes housing, food, photostat, computer, internet, solar, and parlor.

Sources: CDF. *Bangladesh Microfinance Statistics, 2011 to 2019/20*. Dhaka.

Government Role in Financing and Regulating Microfinance

MFIs in Bangladesh have long been offering financial services (e.g., credit, savings, and insurance) to the poor and funding their operations through internally generated funds, such as member savings, which have often been supplemented with bank borrowings. In the 1990s the apex body, Palli Karma Sahayak Foundation (PKSF), was created to support rural development through employment and income generation in the country, which eventually provided seed funds for MFIs to become partner organization of PKSF all over the country.[3] PKSF uses stringent criteria for funding such as business purpose, reputation, credible intent to serve the poor, accounting system, staff size, and loan performance of the MFI. The subsidized loans from PKSF are the major source of finance for its partner organizations (MFIs). The Microcredit Regulatory Authority (MRA) is formally tasked with monitoring the transparency and governance of MFIs, with the governor of Bangladesh Bank being its chairperson.[4] MRA exercises its rights and responsibilities as per the Microcredit Regulatory Authority Act, 2006, enacted by the government. MRA grants licenses to MFIs (including different licensing fees according to number of borrowers of MFIs), undertakes strict monitoring to ensure compliance, and takes necessary punitive action if compliance is broken. Although MRA is the formal authority, other involved authorities in microfinance activities are the Ministry of Finance; Bangladesh Bank; and the Ministry of Local Government, Rural Development, and Cooperatives. As of June 2020, there were 759 MFIs registered with the MRA. These MFIs operate in 20,898 branch offices and have 33.3 million members with 0.17 million employees (MRA Annual Report 2020). The MRA has also set its own rules and issued several circulars, such as prohibiting installments receipt in cyclone-hit areas, establishing minimum fees, lifting collateral requirements, setting a grace period, minimum and maximum interest rates, and so

---

[3] For details on PKSF programs and financing see https://pksf-bd.org/web.
[4] See https://mra.gov.bd.

on (Badruddoza 2013). The expansion of microfinance for the poverty reduction agenda of the government as well as achieving the SDGs is highlighted in the Eighth Five-Year Plan.

Microfinance Institution Surveys in Five Districts: What Do They Say?

We surveyed major MFIs operating in the sample districts. In all the selected villages of five districts during the census, information was collected on MFIs operating in the villages and their associated households. The top three MFIs serving the surveyed households in each village completed a detail survey. The top three are those who have the highest number of subscribers in the villages. The objective of the MFI survey was to collect MFI branch-level administrative as well as financial information in relation to member characteristics.

As some of the MFI branches cover multiple villages in our survey, we administer surveys at the branch level using a computer-assisted personal interviewing questionnaire. Thus, across the five districts we collected data from 285 MFI branches operating in 124 villages. We mainly collect information about branch-level information on manager qualifications and experience, number of MFI members, number of groups, number of borrowers, interest rates, use of MFS for loan disbursement and installment collection, gender-wise and category-wise disbursement, outstanding loans and recovery, and savings-related information.

The top three MFIs in terms of household participation in the selected villages are GB (68), BRAC (65), and ASA (82). Other MFIs also appear among the top three in some villages. The distribution of MFI branches surveyed across each district is provided in **Table 21**. The major MFIs are branches of ASA, BRAC, and GB in all five districts. Across all districts and MFIs, each surveyed branch operates in between 27 and 39 villages.

Table 21: Distribution of Microfinance Institution Branches in Surveyed Districts

MFI	District Name					
---	Dinajpur	Gaibandha	Kurigram	Lalmonirhat	Rangpur	Total
GB	18	11	12	11	16	68
	(27.69)	(17.19)	(25)	(22.45)	(26.67)	(23.78)
BRAC	19	8	11	12	15	65
	(29.23)	(12.5)	(22.92)	(24.49)	(25)	(22.73)
ASA	18	17	14	14	19	82
	(27.69)	(26.56)	(29.17)	(28.57)	(31.67)	(28.67)
BURO	0	1	2	0	1	4
	(0)	(1.56)	(4.17)	(0)	(1.67)	(1.4)
TMSS	2	1	3	3	1	10
	(3.08)	(1.56)	(6.25)	(6.12)	(1.67)	(3.5)
Jagoroni	0	0	0	0	1	1
	(0)	(0)	(0)	(0)	(1.67)	(0.35)
Uddipon	0	0	1	0	1	2
	(0)	(0)	(2.08)	(0)	(1.67)	(0.7)
RDRS	1	1	5	5	0	12
	(1.54)	(1.56)	(10.42)	(10.2)	(0)	(4.2)

continued on next page

Table 21 continued

MFI	District Name					
	Dinajpur	Gaibandha	Kurigram	Lalmonirhat	Rangpur	Total
MBSK	1	0	0	0	0	1
	(1.54)	(0)	(0)	(0)	(0)	(0.35)
Al Falah	1	0	0	0	0	1
	(1.54)	(0)	(0)	(0)	(0)	(0.35)
GUK	1	6	0	0	0	7
	(1.54)	(9.38)	(0)	(0)	(0)	(2.45)
Gram Bikash Kendra	1	0	0	0	1	2
	(1.54)	(0)	(0)	(0)	(1.67)	(0.7)
Heed Bangladesh	2	2	0	0	1	5
	(3.08)	(3.13)	(0)	(0)	(1.67)	(1.75)
SKS Foundation	1	15	0	1	3	20
	(1.54)	(23.44)	(0)	(2.04)	(5)	(6.99)
Bij	0	2	0	0	0	2
	(0)	(3.13)	(0)	(0)	(0)	(0.7)
Nazir	0	0	0	1	0	1
	(0)	(0)	(0)	(2.04)	(0)	(0.35)
POPI	0	0	0	2	0	2
	(0)	(0)	(0)	(4.08)	(0)	(0.7)
Light House	0	0	0	0	1	1
	(0)	(0)	(0)	(0)	(1.67)	(0.35)
Total	65	64	48	49	60	286
	(100)	(100)	(100)	(100)	(100)	(100)

GB = Grameen Bank, MFI = microfinance institution.

Note: Figures in parentheses are share of MFI branches among all MFIs in a district.

Source: Authors' calculations based on the ADB–BIDS Digital Microcredit Survey 2021.

Profile of Microfinance Institution Branch Managers

The average age of surveyed branch managers is 42–44 years in the surveyed districts. The majority of branch managers are male with an education level of master's degree or higher (over 58%), while others have completed a bachelor's degree (almost 35%) and a few have completed higher secondary education (about 7%). On average, managers reported being with the surveyed branch for 2.0–2.5 years. Their average overall job experience varies by district between 16.5 years to almost 20.0 years, and their experience in the MFI sector is on average between 15.4 years and 19.0 years.

We first show basic statistics of MFI members, borrowers, interest rates, yearly branch operating costs, outstanding loans, and recovery rates with respect to three major MFIs (**Table 22**). The highest average number of members and borrowers are with GB, which offers the lowest average interest on savings among the three MFIs, and charges the highest average interest on loans for manufacturing and business activities, though the lowest for service activities. The yearly cost of branch operations is also highest on average for GB branches, twice as much as the other two MFIs. Total outstanding loans across gender does not match with total outstanding across sector, since not all MFI branches keep this data disaggregated by both gender and sector. Average recovery rates exceed 91%, except for ASA in 2019–2020 when it dropped to around 90%.

Table 22: Survey Findings from Select Variables in Major Microfinance Institutions

Indicators	Grameen Bank		BRAC		ASA	
	Mean	SD	Mean	SD	Mean	SD
Total members	4,667 (N = 68)	1,455	3,493 (N = 65)	1799	2,658 (N = 80)	350
Total current borrowers	3,074 (N = 68)	1,183	2,399 (N = 65)	912	2,390 (N = 82)	312
Interest rate on member savings (annual %)	5.04 (N = 68)	0.18	6.02 (N = 65)	0.70	6.06 (N = 81)	0.56
Interest rate on loans for manufacturing activities (annual %)	15.93 (N = 60)	4.89	12.56 (N = 54)	2.32	11.83 (N = 69)	1.46
Interest rate on loans for service activities (annual %)	6.11 (N = 60)	3.18	12.42 (N = 46)	1.52	11.51 (N = 77)	1.85
Interest rate on loans for business and trade activities (annual %)	16.11 (N = 68)	4.85	12.20 (N = 64)	2.44	12.40 (N = 82)	0.92
Yearly cost of branch operations (Tk million)	10.90 (N = 68)	8.36	4.29 (N = 62)	2.39	5.64 (N = 82)	5.63
Total outstanding loans, across gender (FY2021) (Tk million)	10.60 (N = 66)	17.00	24.80 (N = 65)	113.00	15.50 (N = 82)	22.80
Total outstanding loans, across sector (FY2021) (Tk million)	10.30 (N = 66)	20.30	10.30 (N = 65)	18.00	19.40 (N = 82)	47.70
Total outstanding loans, across gender (FY2020) (Tk million)	11.10 (N = 66)	18.40	8.99 (N = 65)	13.40	14.70 (N = 82)	19.40
Total outstanding loans, across sector (FY2020) (Tk million)	5.96 (N = 66)	8.93	9.13 (N = 65)	13.50	14.60 (N = 82)	18.80
Total outstanding loans, across gender (FY2019)	10.00 (N = 64)	19.50	6.53 (N = 64)	13.20	11.00 (N = 82)	20.20
Total outstanding loans, across sector (FY2019) (Tk million)	6.92 (N = 64)	15.30	6.87 (N = 64)	14.80	11.20 (N = 82)	20.20
Average recovery rate, across gender (FY2021)	91.84 (N = 65)	9.76	91.46 (N = 62)	5.68	91.64 (N = 75)	5.37
Average recovery rate, across categories (FY2021)	92.53 (N = 66)	9.87	92.11 (N = 62)	5.56	92.65 (N = 73)	4.68
Average recovery rate, across gender (FY2020)	93.12 (N = 64)	6.46	92.03 (N = 62)	5.50	89.54 (N = 75)	5.98
Average recovery rate, across categories (FY2020)	92.99 (N = 64)	7.83	92.34 (N = 62)	5.36	90.72 (N = 72)	5.55
Average recovery rate, across gender (FY2019)	95.54 (N = 63)	5.88	95.78 (N = 62)	3.89	95.71 (N = 75)	3.69
Average recovery rate, across categories (FY2019)	95.01 (N = 63)	8.34	95.99 (N = 63)	4.00	96.32 (N = 72)	3.55

FY= fiscal year, SD = standard deviation.

Note: Major is defined by the proportion of total microfinance institutions in surveyed villages that respondents are member of.

Source: Authors' calculations based on the ADB–BIDS Digital Microcredit Survey 2021.

Market Shares of Major Microfinance Institutions

Table 23 shows the district-wise shares of major MFIs for total loans disbursed and outstanding loans. GB accounts for the major share of disbursed loans in Dinajpur district, although it declines from about 53% to 49% over the last 3 years of the review period. On the other hand, ASA claims the major share of loans disbursed in the remaining four districts. With respect to outstanding loans, we see some differences across districts among these major MFIs in terms of percentage share. We also see that in the case of GB, overall loan disbursement in the surveyed districts decreased in 2020/21 due to COVID-19, while outstanding loans increased in Rangpur and Dinajpur district compared with the other three districts covered in the study. In case of the other two MFIs, the trends in loan disbursement as well as the outstanding loan situation are rather mixed in 2020/21. While BRAC disbursed less in Dinajpur, Rangpur, and Gaibandha, it increased disbursement in Kurigram and Lalmonirhat, where outstanding loans increased in 2020/21 compared with the previous year. ASA also saw higher disbursement in Dinajpur, Kurigram, Lalmonirhat and Rangpur in 2020/21; its outstanding loans only decreased in Dinajpur in 2020/21 compared with previous years.

Table 23: Percent of Disbursed and Outstanding Loans by District
(Major Microfinance Institutions)

District		Grameen Bank			BRAC			ASA		
		2018/19	2019/20	2020/21	2018/19	2019/20	2020/21	2018/19	2019/20	2020/21
Dinajpur	Disbursed	52.81	49.32	48.50	17.61	17.79	17.93	21.21	23.74	24.57
	Outstanding	24.35	14.59	31.11	24.97	25.57	41.56	39.39	29.96	23.33
Gaibandha	Disbursed	17.86	17.73	17.10	10.00	8.80	9.30	31.72	37.79	28.98
	Outstanding	13.47	8.26	10.87	16.33	15.56	9.49	34.13	34.73	43.68
Kurigram	Disbursed	27.03	25.26	20.65	22.03	23.31	24.31	35.68	36.17	40.56
	Outstanding	40.39	27.29	29.05	25.83	22.88	28.77	13.94	33.31	25.77
Lalmonirhat	Disbursed	25.26	22.47	25.61	21.95	28.19	24.34	33.43	30.32	32.68
	Outstanding	33.71	14.00	15.47	24.95	24.00	34.49	24.57	48.34	27.98
Rangpur	Disbursed	30.37	31.39	29.91	22.09	24.03	24.33	36.29	33.12	37.28
	Outstanding	21.95	18.32	33.42	9.22	20.98	17.54	58.75	44.61	38.77

Source: Authors' calculations based on the ADB–BIDS Digital Microcredit Survey 2021.

The sector-wise average loan disbursement of major MFIs from 2018/19 to 2020/21 is shown in **Table 24**. GB disbursed the largest amount of loans on average for manufacturing activities, disbursing Tk19.8 million in 2018–2019, which dropped to Tk19.0 million in 2019/20 and shot up to Tk24.7 million in 2020/21. For business activities, all three MFIs' average disbursements were roughly similar in each of the 3 years under review, with ASA having the highest (Tk13.8 million, Tk12.5 million, and Tk14.6 million, respectively). For loans by category, general microcredit had the highest average disbursement across all three major MFIs, with GB having the highest: Tk62.3 million, Tk54.4 million, and Tk50.7 million in 2018–2019, 2019–2020, and 2020–2021, respectively. This, however, showed a declining trend in average loan disbursement for general microcredit activities for GB, whereas for BRAC there was a slight drop and then an increase, and for ASA there was an increase and then a decrease.

Table 24: Average Loan Disbursement of Major Microfinance Institutions by Sector

MFI	Sector	2018/19 (Tk million)		2019/20 (Tk million)		2020/21 (Tk million)	
		Mean	SD	Mean	SD	Mean	SD
GB	Manufacturing	19.8 (N = 61)	38.500	19 (N = 61)	39.100	24.7 (N = 61)	46.100
	Service	0.853 (N = 55)	2.504	0.973 (N = 55)	2.632	0.859 (N = 51)	2.544
	Business	12.2 (N = 64)	14.000	11.2 (N = 64)	13.400	10.8 (N = 64)	11.800
	General microcredit	62.3 (N = 62)	47.000	54.4 (N = 62)	42.700	50.7 (N = 62)	34.900
	Agriculture	8.869 (N = 57)	17.800	9.515 (N = 59)	18.500	9.721 (N = 59)	18.500
	Education	0.841 (N = 59)	3.378	0.798 (N = 58)	2.996	0.712 (N = 58)	3.151
	Housebuilding	1.586 (N = 63)	5.138	1.094 (N = 63)	2.469	1.304 (N = 59)	3.212
	Seasonal	4.524 (N = 61)	6.385	3.701 (N = 61)	4.614	3.428 (N = 58)	4.119
	Emergency	0.111 (N = 54)	0.604	0.119 (N = 56)	0.802	0.177 (N = 54)	0.907
	Other	0.01 (N = 54)	0.068	0.011 (N = 55)	0.058	0.014 (N = 53)	0.067
BRAC	Manufacturing	1.749 (N = 59)	6.329	1.884 (N = 60)	7.141	2.015 (N = 59)	8.170
	Service	1.159 (N = 53)	2.401	2.242 (N = 55)	9.307	2.526 (N = 55)	6.799
	Business	8.115 (N = 64)	7.977	8.065 (N = 64)	7.682	10 (N = 64)	19.500
	General microcredit	27.1 (N = 63)	23.800	26.9 (N = 63)	22.400	28.6 (N = 63)	24.600
	Agriculture	22.6 (N = 64)	28.000	23.7 (N = 65)	30.700	19.6 (N = 65)	20.300
	Education	0.266 (N = 54)	1.227	0.313 (N = 54)	1.468	1.941 (N = 54)	12.200
	Housebuilding	0.78 (N = 56)	2.613	0.707 (N = 55)	2.300	0.819 (N = 56)	2.620
	Seasonal	2.455 (N = 55)	5.078	1.863 (N = 56)	4.435	2.6 (N = 56)	5.291
	Emergency	0.227 (N = 54)	1.442	0.563 (N = 55)	2.311	0.241 (N = 55)	1.482
	Other	0 (N = 53)	0.000	0 (N = 53)	0.000	0 (N = 52)	0.000
ASA	Manufacturing	1.998 (N = 78)	6.728	1.125 (N = 78)	1.977	1.35 (N = 78)	2.217
	Service	3.367 (N = 72)	7.449	2.809 (N = 72)	7.262	3.644 (N = 72)	8.339
	Business	13.8 (N = 82)	11.400	12.5 (N = 82)	10.100	14.6 (N = 82)	11.400
	General microcredit	32.9 (N = 82)	26.700	36.7 (N = 82)	67.300	33.6 (N = 82)	26.600
	Agriculture	27.4 (N = 82)	22.100	26.4 (N = 82)	19.900	28.4 (N = 82)	22.600
	Education	0.497 (N = 76)	1.143	0.495 (N = 74)	1.226	0.604 (N = 76)	1.514

continued on next page

Table 24 continued

MFI	Sector	2018/19 (Tk million)		2019/20 (Tk million)		2020/21 (Tk million)	
		Mean	SD	Mean	SD	Mean	SD
	Housebuilding	0.624 (N = 70)	1.252	0.56 (N = 71)	1.304	0.618 (N = 72)	1.290
	Seasonal	4.018 (N = 75)	6.171	3.521 (N = 76)	5.495	4.373 (N = 76)	6.795
	Emergency	0.156 (N = 67)	0.523	0.132 (N = 69)	0.498	0.156 (N = 69)	0.570
	Other	0.513 (N = 70)	1.998	0.501 (N = 72)	2.147	0.608 (N = 73)	2.596

GB = Grameen Bank, MFI = microfinance institution, SD = standard deviation.

Note: Major is defined by the proportion of total MFIs in surveyed villages that respondents are member of.

Source: Authors' calculations based on the ADB–BIDS Digital Microcredit Survey 2021.

Table 25 shows the average loans outstanding by sector and category as in Table 24, but for all MFIs and for each district. General microcredit and agriculture loans seem to have the highest average disbursement during the review period for all districts in general. The highest average disbursements for general microcredit and agriculture were in Gaibandha, whereas the lowest average disbursements in the other four districts ranged from Tk0.5 million to Tk3.3 million in general microcredit, and from Tk0.5 million to Tk3.0 million in agriculture. Average disbursements for Gaibandha district range from Tk13.7 million to almost Tk16.0 million in general microcredit, and from almost Tk9.0 million to over Tk11.0 million in agriculture.

Table 25: Average Loans Outstanding by Sector and District for All Microfinance Institutions

District	Sector	2018/19 (Tk million)		2019/20 (Tk million)		2020/21 (Tk million)	
		Mean	SD	Mean	SD	Mean	SD
Dinajpur	Manufacturing	0.272 (N = 63)	1.216	0.282 (N = 64)	0.795	0.208 (N = 64)	0.663
	Service	0.04 (N = 63)	0.182	0.023 (N = 63)	0.089	0.018 (N = 63)	0.049
	Business	0.452 (N = 64)	0.659	0.775 (N = 63)	0.938	1.979 (N = 64)	8.508
	General microcredit	0.52 (N = 63)	0.746	1.028 (N = 64)	2.471	0.934 (N = 64)	1.186
	Agriculture	0.853 (N = 64)	1.173	1.689 (N = 63)	3.545	3.113 (N = 63)	11.2
	Education	0.013 (N = 61)	0.038	0.018 (N = 64)	0.047	0.456 (N = 63)	3.41
	Housebuilding	0.044 (N = 62)	0.113	0.048 (N = 63)	0.145	0.052 (N = 62)	0.133
	Seasonal	0.096 (N = 64)	0.345	0.125 (N = 64)	0.278	0.305 (N = 62)	1.52
	Emergency	0.000* (N = 63)	0.003	0.000 (N = 62)	0	0.005 (N = 62)	0.04
	Other	0.019 (N = 62)	0.152	0.033 (N = 63)	0.251	0.025 (N = 62)	0.194

continued on next page

Table 25 continued

District	Sector	2018/19 (Tk million)		2019/20 (Tk million)		2020/21 (Tk million)	
		Mean	SD	Mean	SD	Mean	SD
Gaibandha	Manufacturing	1.779 (N = 54)	11.7	0.199 (N = 56)	0.596	1.59 (N = 59)	10.5
	Service	0.635 (N = 55)	1.763	0.568 (N = 56)	1.482	0.539 (N = 59)	1.055
	Business	4.992 (N = 59)	5.245	5.329 (N = 58)	5.447	5.706 (N = 60)	6.076
	General microcredit	13.7 (N = 57)	14.9	15.7 (N = 59)	16.1	15.9 (N = 60)	15.6
	Agriculture	8.913 (N = 55)	13.1	8.944 (N = 56)	13.8	11.3 (N = 58)	14.6
	Education	0.302 (N = 53)	1.152	0.175 (N = 55)	0.354	0.19 (N = 58)	0.468
	Housebuilding	0.47 (N = 53)	1.032	0.483 (N = 56)	1.029	0.605 (N = 58)	1.149
	Seasonal	1.736 (N = 51)	3.112	1.744 (N = 55)	3.468	7.783 (N = 59)	44.1
	Emergency	0.688 (N = 50)	1.658	0.673 (N = 54)	1.639	0.789 (N = 57)	1.696
	Other	0.527 (N = 49)	1.488	0.71 (N = 51)	2.516	0.937 (N = 54)	2.671
Kurigram	Manufacturing	1.881 (N = 19)	4.66	1.657 (N = 22)	3.585	2.143 (N = 22)	4.145
	Service	0.058 (N = 6)	0.057	0.116 (N = 6)	0.111	0.122 (N = 6)	0.121
	Business	0.186 (N = 38)	0.235	0.627 (N = 40)	1.064	0.63 (N = 38)	0.954
	General microcredit	1.133 (N = 38)	1.393	2.461 (N = 37)	2.702	2.596 (N = 38)	2.85
	Agriculture	1.055 (N = 36)	1.767	2.095 (N = 37)	2.667	1.996 (N = 38)	2.458
	Education	0.094 (N = 4)	0.155	0.006 (N = 3)	0.01	0.06 (N = 4)	0.115
	Housebuilding	0.088 (N = 5)	0.171	0.172 (N = 7)	0.293	0.218 (N = 9)	0.545
	Seasonal	0.152 (N = 11)	0.178	0.246 (N = 12)	0.257	0.262 (N = 12)	0.484
	Emergency	0.094 (N = 3)	0.1	0.153 (N = 3)	0.213	0.251 (N = 3)	0.421
	Other	0.051 (N = 3)	0.051	0.064 (N = 6)	0.073	0.041 (N = 6)	0.034
Lalmonirhat	Manufacturing	0.022 (N = 26)	0.069	0.08 (N = 27)	0.237	0.066 (N = 27)	0.164
	Service	0.018 (N = 25)	0.081	0.028 (N = 30)	0.127	0.052 (N = 27)	0.183
	Business	0.394 (N = 48)	0.927	0.596 (N = 48)	0.837	0.825 (N = 48)	1.722
	General microcredit	1.343 (N = 49)	1.461	2.353 (N = 49)	2.051	3.362 (N = 49)	2.477

continued on next page

Table 25 continued

District	Sector	2018/19 (Tk million)		2019/20 (Tk million)		2020/21 (Tk million)	
		Mean	SD	Mean	SD	Mean	SD
	Agriculture	0.414 (N = 37)	0.667	0.645 (N = 37)	0.87	0.759 (N = 39)	0.809
	Education	0.08 (N = 19)	0.341	0.004 (N = 17)	0.012	0.049 (N = 22)	0.191
	Housebuilding	0.012 (N = 24)	0.034	0.017 (N = 25)	0.049	0.021 (N = 26)	0.064
	Seasonal	0.069 (N = 29)	0.268	0.136 (N = 30)	0.397	0.128 (N = 30)	0.353
	Emergency	0 (N = 9)	0	0 (N = 10)	0	0 (N = 12)	0
	Other	0 (N = 1)	–	0 (N = 2)	0	0 (N = 7)	0
Rangpur	Manufacturing	0.005 (N = 58)	0.026	0.197 (N = 59)	1.458	0.05 (N = 60)	0.38
	Service	0.157 (N = 58)	0.286	0.502 (N = 59)	0.826	0.259 (N = 60)	0.397
	Business	0.416 (N = 58)	0.535	1.379 (N = 59)	1.342	0.932 (N = 60)	1.088
	General microcredit	1.467 (N = 58)	2.448	3.22 (N = 59)	2.406	3.22 (N = 60)	5.806
	Agriculture	1.913 (N = 58)	9.016	3.199 (N = 59)	3.501	1.623 (N = 60)	1.749
	Education	0.056 (N = 57)	0.145	0.08 (N = 59)	0.209	0.057 (N = 60)	0.178
	Housebuilding	0.009 (N = 58)	0.056	0.043 (N = 59)	0.171	0.014 (N = 60)	0.06
	Seasonal	0.24 (N = 57)	1.59	0.355 (N = 56)	1.498	0.067 (N = 60)	0.166
	Emergency	0.000* (N = 58)	0.002	0.000 (N = 58)	0	0.001 (N = 60)	0.008
	Other	0.166 (N = 58)	1.267	0.016 (N = 59)	0.12	0.009 (N = 60)	0.073

SD = standard deviation.

Note: Emergency loans were not usually found in the surveyed branches of Dinajpur and Rangpur.

Source: Authors' calculations based on the ADB–BIDS Digital Microcredit Survey 2021.

Next, we look at the trends in total loans disbursed (by sector) and total outstanding (by sector) for 2018/19 to 2020/21 for all MFIs across all districts combined, then by each of the five districts, and then the same for each of the major three MFIs. Total loans disbursed show a similar trend for all MFIs as well as for the major three MFIs (GB, BRAC, an ASA) (**Figure 5** and **Figure 6**). Total disbursement for all MFIs dropped in 2019–2020 from Tk22.0 billion to Tk21.3 billion, before rising to Tk21.9 billion in 2020–2021. If we look at this district-wise, we see Rangpur's disbursements are rising over the review period, while Lalmonirhat's declined over the same period. Both Dinajpur's and Kurigram's fell in 2019–2020 but rose again in the next year. Though Kurigram's total disbursement was lowest of all five districts, the declining trend of Lalmonirhat and rising trend of Kurigram meant that Lalmonirhat surveyed branches ended up with the lowest total disbursements as of 2020/21. Gaibandha had the highest disbursement until 2019/20, but then dropped below Rangpur and Dinajpur.

Figure 5: Trend in Loans Disbursed across All Microfinance Institutions

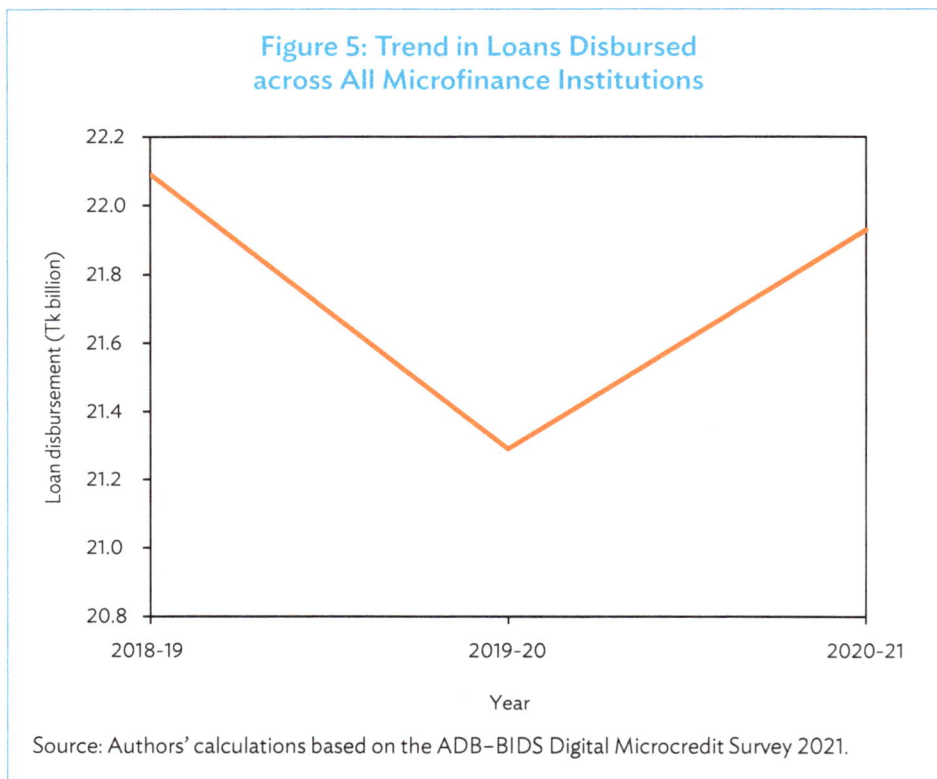

Source: Authors' calculations based on the ADB–BIDS Digital Microcredit Survey 2021.

Figure 6: Trend in Loans Disbursed by District for All Microfinance Institutions

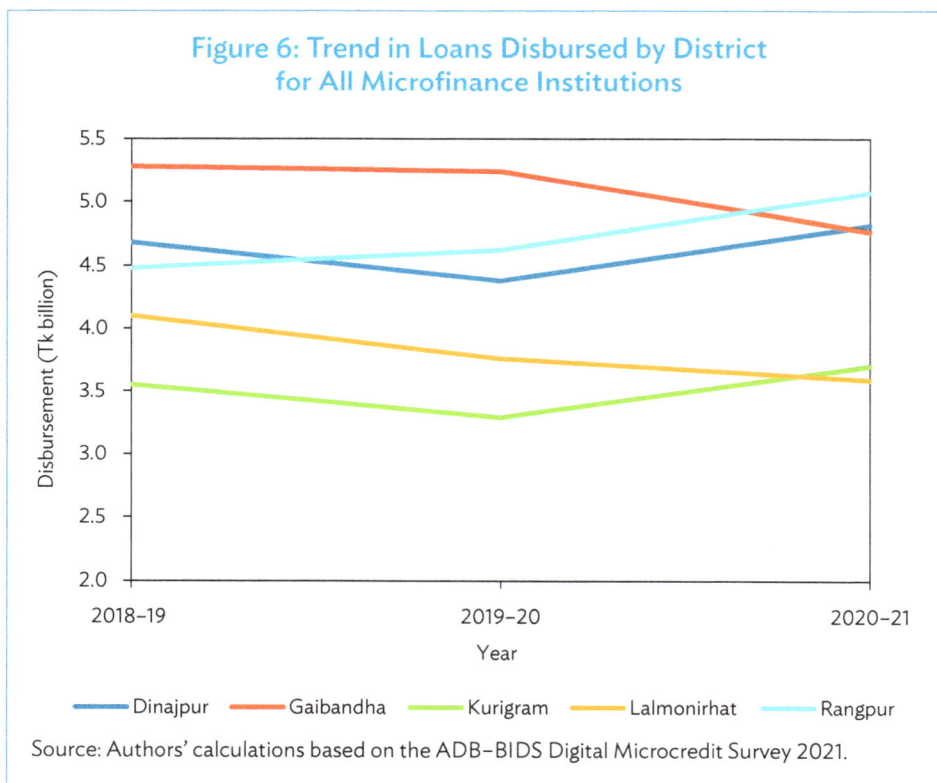

Source: Authors' calculations based on the ADB–BIDS Digital Microcredit Survey 2021.

As mentioned earlier, the three major MFIs show a similar trend in disbursement as all MFIs (**Figure 7**). When we break this down by each of the three MFIs, we see that GB- and ASA-surveyed branches had similar disbursements in 2018–2019, but GB's disbursements fell the next year before increasing slightly (**Figure 8**). BRAC-surveyed branches' disbursements had been the lowest but increased over the years (though remained much lower than the other two MFIs' branches).

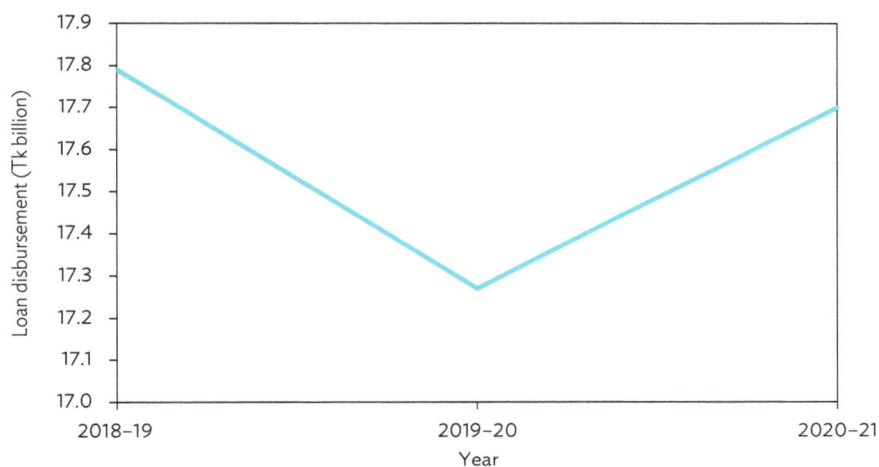

Figure 7: Trend in Loans Disbursed across Major Microfinance Institutions

Source: Authors' calculations based on the ADB–BIDS Digital Microcredit Survey 2021.

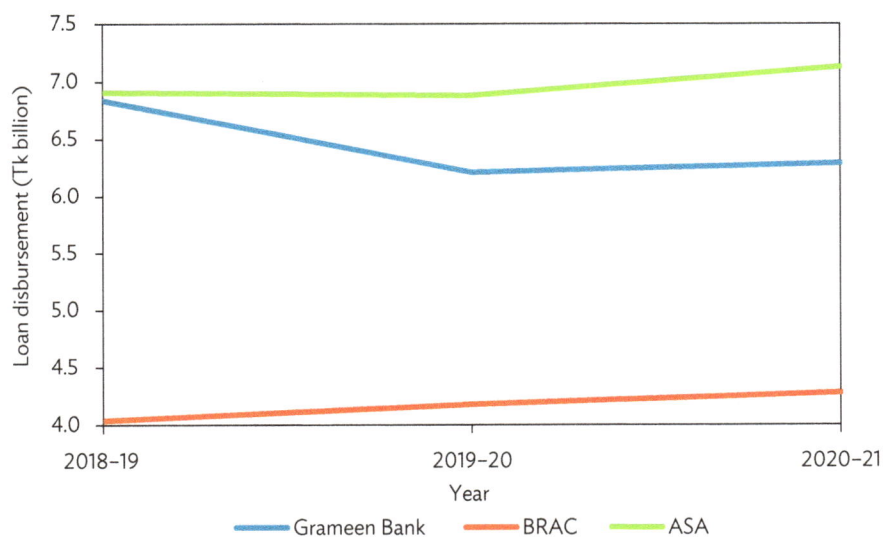

Figure 8: Trend in Loans Disbursed by Major Microfinance Institutions

Source: Authors' calculations based on the ADB–BIDS Digital Microcredit Survey 2021.

When we look at the total loans outstanding, we observe that it has a steadily rising trend for all MFIs as well as for the major three ones (**Figure 9** and **Figure 10**). Looking at the district-wise trends for all MFIs, Gaibandha has far higher loans outstanding than the other districts and the growth picks up more after 2019/20. Surveyed branches in Kurigram and Lalmonirhat had very similar outstanding amounts during the review period. Dinajpur's outstanding loans increased after 2019/20 and surpassed Rangpur's, which dropped despite having been higher in both 2018/19 and 2019/20.

Figure 9: Trend in Loans Outstanding across All Microfinance Institutions

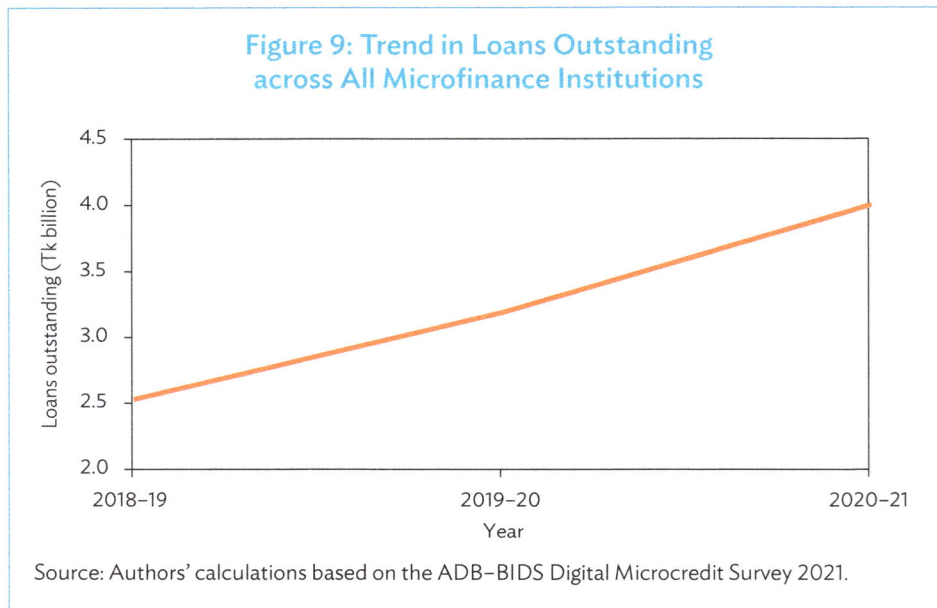

Source: Authors' calculations based on the ADB–BIDS Digital Microcredit Survey 2021.

Figure 10: Trend in Loans Outstanding by District for All Microfinance Institutions

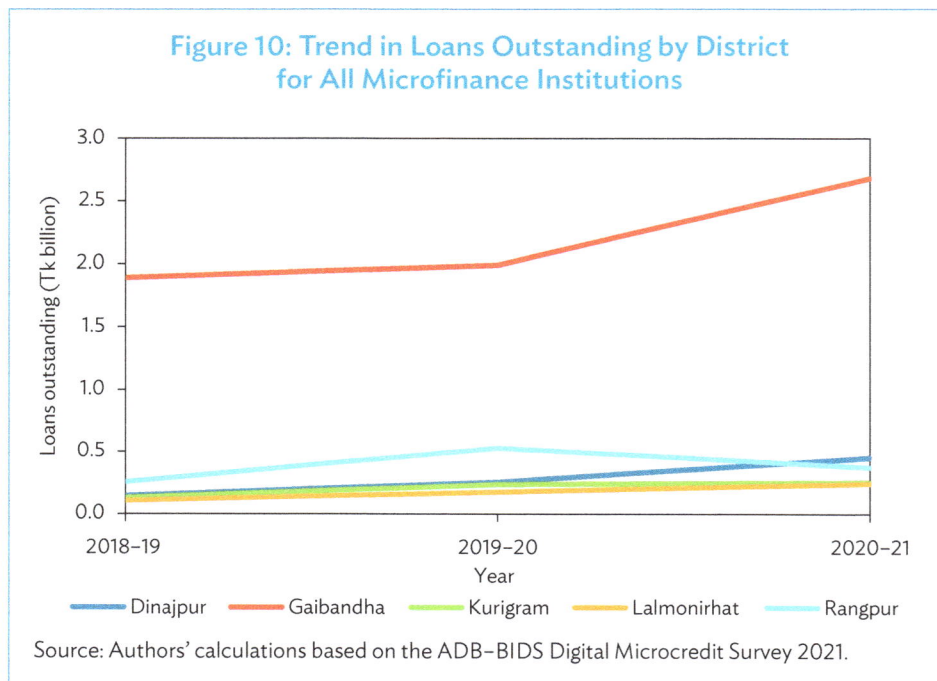

Source: Authors' calculations based on the ADB–BIDS Digital Microcredit Survey 2021.

Figure 11 shows that ASA branches' outstanding amounts were the highest among the three major MFIs in 2018/19 and increased further after 2019/20. GB and BRAC had similar amounts in 2018/19. GB's decreased in 2019/20 before rising again, though BRAC's had continued rising albeit at a slower pace.

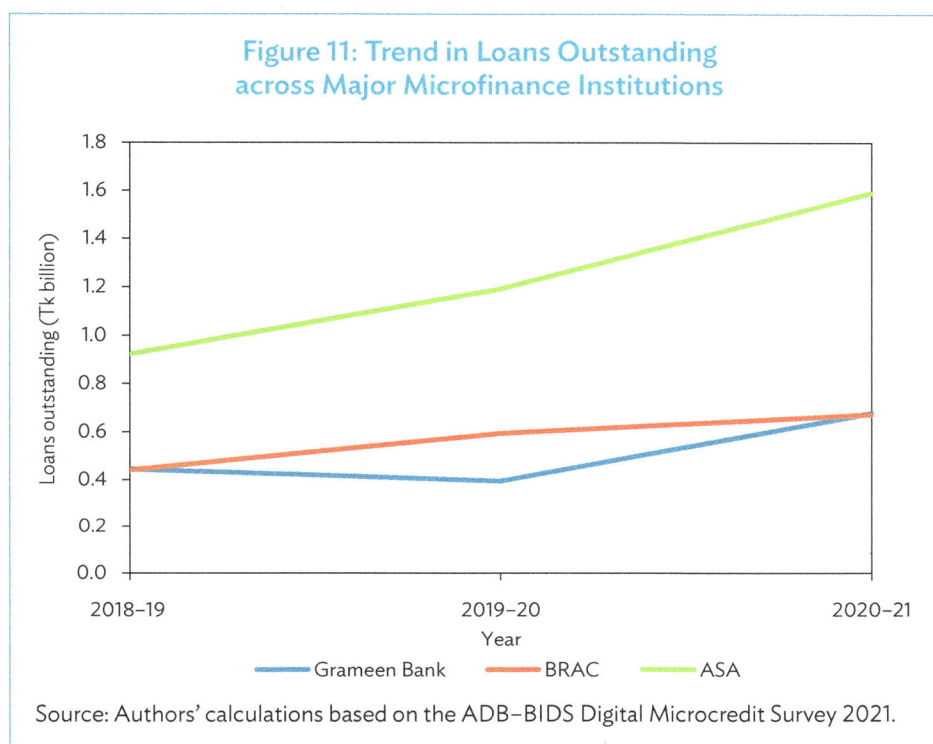

Figure 11: Trend in Loans Outstanding across Major Microfinance Institutions

Source: Authors' calculations based on the ADB–BIDS Digital Microcredit Survey 2021.

The distribution of average interest rate on member savings offered by these three major MFIs (GB, BRAC, and ASA) in each of the districts is given in **Table 26**. We observe that the interest rate for borrower deposits is roughly similar across districts but slightly higher for BRAC and ASA compared with GB.

Table 26: Interest Rates of Major Microfinance Institutions on Borrowers Savings by District

Interest Rate on Savings	Grameen Bank		BRAC		ASA	
District	Mean	SD	Mean	SD	Mean	SD
Dinajpur	5.00 (N = 18)	0	5.89 (N = 19)	1.100	6.17 (N = 18)	1.150
Gaibandha	5.00 (N = 11)	0	6.38 (N = 8)	1.061	6.09 (N = 17)	0.364
Kurigram	5.13 (N = 12)	0.311	6.00 (N = 11)	0	6.00 (N = 14)	0
Lalmonirhat	5.00 (N = 11)	0	6.00 (N = 12)	0	6.00 (N = 14)	0
Rangpur	5.06 (N = 16)	0.250	6.00 (N = 15)	0	6.00 (N = 18)	0

SD = standard deviation.

Source: Authors' calculations based on the ADB–BIDS Digital Microcredit Survey 2021.

Interest Rates and Savings

We then report the average interest rate offered by major MFIs on loans for manufacturing (**Table 27**), services (**Table 28**), and business activities (**Table 29**) in each surveyed district. Next, we report various savings by borrowers with MFIs.

Interest rates vary by MFIs as well as by districts. On loans for manufacturing activities, GB charges between 17% and 20% interest rates in Dinajpur (20%), Lalmonirhat (18%), Rangpur (17%), and much lower in Kurigram (10%) and Gaibandha (12%). However, the other two MFIs, BRAC and ASA, roughly charge similar interest rates across all five districts (between 11% and 12%) for loans for manufacturing activities.

Table 27: Interest Rates of Major Microfinance Institutions on Loans for Manufacturing Activities

District	Grameen Bank		BRAC		ASA	
	Mean	SD	Mean	SD	Mean	SD
Dinajpur	20.00 (N = 17)	0	12.59 (N = 18)	2.431	12.26 (N = 18)	1.603
Gaibandha	12.22 (N = 9)	4.410	13.50 (N = 7)	4.646	10.96 (N = 12)	1.484
Kurigram	10.00 (N = 12)	0	12.32 (N = 11)	0.252	11.16 (N = 14)	1.447
Lalmonirhat	18.33 (N = 6)	4.082	12.00 (N = 5)	0	11.63 (N = 12)	1.110
Rangpur	17.22 (N = 16)	4.332	12.42 (N = 13)	1.935	12.96 (N = 13)	0.139

SD = standard deviation.

Source: Authors' calculations based on the ADB–BIDS Digital Microcredit Survey 2021.

The average interest rate offered by major MFIs on loans for service activities is shown in Table 28. Interestingly, GB charges much lower rates on average than the other two MFIs. However, charges roughly double the interest rate for service activities in Rangpur compared with other districts (16% versus 6%–8%). Interestingly, GB charges much lower rate on average than the other two MFIs.

Table 28: Interest Rates of Major Microfinance Institutions on Loans for Service Activities

District	Grameen Bank		BRAC		ASA	
	Mean	SD	Mean	SD	Mean	SD
Dinajpur	7.50 (N = 12)	5.839	12.01 (N = 17)	2.386	10.72 (N = 16)	1.291
Gaibandha	7.10 (N = 10)	2.331	15.00 (N = 1)	–	10.24 (N = 17)	3.011
Kurigram	5.45 (N = 11)	1.508	12.36 (N = 11)	0.234	12.39 (N = 14)	0.289
Lalmonirhat	6.36 (N = 11)	1.567	12.25 (N = 2)	0.354	11.36 (N = 11)	0.924
Rangpur	6.59 (N = 16)	2.57	12.77 (N = 15)	0.320	12.76 (N = 19)	0.386

SD = standard deviation.

Source: Authors' calculations based on the ADB–BIDS Digital Microcredit Survey 2021.

For interest rate on loans for business activities, we observe some differences across districts and MFIs. For example, GB charges higher interest rates on loans for business activities in Dinajpur (20%), Lalmonirhat (19%), and Rangpur (17%), compared with Gaibandha (12%) and Kurigram (10%). BRAC, however, charges roughly similar (slightly over 12%) in all districts but Gaibandha (9%). ASA charges roughly similar (12%–13%) interest rate on average in each district.

Table 29: Average Interest Rates of Major Microfinance Institutions on Loans for Business Activities

District	Grameen Bank		BRAC		ASA	
	Mean	SD	Mean	SD	Mean	SD
Dinajpur	20.00 (N = 18)	0	12.90 (N = 19)	1.751	12.12 (N = 18)	1.679
Gaibandha	11.82 (N = 11)	4.045	8.94 (N = 8)	5.519	12.26 (N = 17)	0.812
Kurigram	10.00 (N = 12)	0	12.41 (N = 11)	0.202	12.43 (N = 14)	0.267
Lalmonirhat	19.09 (N = 11)	3.015	12.18 (N = 11)	0.462	12.29 (N = 14)	0.469
Rangpur	17.22 (N = 16)	4.332	12.93 (N = 15)	0.176	12.87 (N = 19)	0.226

SD = standard deviation.

Source: Authors' calculations based on the ADB–BIDS Digital Microcredit Survey 2021.

We observe two kinds of savings that members have with MFI accounts: forced savings (**Table 30**) and voluntary savings (**Table 31**). Female borrowers have substantially higher savings, not surprisingly. We also observe that average savings in some districts declined during the COVID-19 pandemic; this is similar for both types of savings. The Rangpur district branches saw the largest decline in female savings in this context.

Table 30: Average Forced Savings by Gender and District for All Microfinance Institutions
(Tk million)

District	Gender	2018/19		2019/20		2020/21	
		Mean	SD	Mean	SD	Mean	SD
Dinajpur	Male	0.355 (N = 63)	0.354 (N = 63)	0.707	0.718	0.369 (N = 63)	0.734
	Female	9.792 (N = 64)	8.955 (N = 64)	16.100	19.000	8.723 (N = 64)	16.000
Gaibandha	Male	0.596 (N = 56)	2.048 (N = 56)	11.200	1.234	1.044 (N = 56)	3.821
	Female	3.721 (N = 56)	4.522 (N = 56)	5.293	4.439	4.028 (N = 56)	4.676
Kurigram	Male	0.429 (N = 21)	0.417 (N = 21)	0.349	0.314	0.426 (N = 21)	0.365
	Female	3.463 (N = 34)	2.952 (N = 34)	1.450	1.346	3.077 (N = 35)	1.622
Lalmonirhat	Male	1.438 (N = 29)	0.586 (N = 29)	0.840	5.180	0.763 (N = 30)	1.175
	Female	1.941 (N = 47)	1.876 (N = 48)	3.723	3.559	2.246 (N = 48)	4.274
Rangpur	Male	0.436 (N = 59)	0.342 (N = 59)	0.379	0.526	0.393 (N = 59)	0.609
	Female	3.53 (N = 59)	4.265 (N = 59)	6.608	2.548	2.567 (N = 59)	1.799

SD = standard deviation.

Source: Authors' calculations based on the ADB–BIDS Digital Microcredit Survey 2021.

Table 31: Average Voluntary Savings by Gender and District All Microfinance Institutions
(Tk million)

District	Gender	2018/19		2019/20		2020/21	
		Mean	SD	Mean	SD	Mean	SD
Dinajpur	Male	0.545 (N = 63)	0.877	0.846 (N = 63)	2.782	0.487 (N = 62)	0.785
	Female	13.3 (N = 64)	19.600	11.4 (N = 64)	11.600	12.4 (N = 64)	14.600
Gaibandha	Male	1.514 (N = 56)	3.652	1.225 (N = 56)	2.446	1.477 (N = 57)	3.451
	Female	10.8 (N = 59)	18.000	10.1 (N = 59)	15.300	10.4 (N = 60)	16.400
Kurigram	Male	6.786 (N = 26)	27.200	6.075 (N = 25)	23.800	6.667 (N = 25)	25.700
	Female	12.1 (N = 46)	25.300	10.7 (N = 45)	19.500	12.2 (N = 45)	20.800
Lalmonirhat	Male	2.72 (N = 29)	3.517	3.091 (N = 30)	3.802	2.856 (N = 30)	3.671
	Female	11.8 (N = 49)	10.600	12.6 (N = 48)	11.200	16.5 (N = 49)	30.400
Rangpur	Male	0.329 (N = 59)	0.620	0.379 (N = 59)	1.107	0.335 (N = 60)	0.627
	Female	4.991 (N = 59)	6.566	7.889 (N = 59)	33.100	4.553 (N = 59)	5.552

SD = standard deviation.

Source: Authors' calculations based on the ADB–BIDS Digital Microcredit Survey 2021.

Digitalization of Microfinance

To understand the extent of digitalization of loan activities, we asked several questions. Surveyed MFIs are yet to widely employ digitalization as only a few branches in Gaibandha district—BRAC, ASA, Heed Bangladesh, and SKS Foundation—use MFS for disbursing loans. However, 34% of the branches of all surveyed MFIs report loan collections through MFS (**Table 32**). This percentage varies by district from 14% in Gaibandha to 24% in Rangpur.

Table 32: Does the Microfinance Institution Branch Accept Payments through Mobile Financial Services?
(number and percentage)

MFS	Dinajpur	Gaibandha	Kurigram	Lalmonirhat	Rangpur	Total
Yes	15	14	23	23	24	99
	(23.08)	(22.22)	(47.92)	(46.94)	(40)	(34.74)
No	50	49	25	26	36	186
	(76.92)	(77.78)	(52.08)	(53.06)	(60)	(65.26)
Total	65	63	48	49	60	285
	(100)	(100)	(100)	(100)	(100)	(100)

MFS = mobile financial services.

Note: Data for all microfinance institutions.

Source: Authors' calculations based on the ADB–BIDS Digital Microcredit Survey 2021.

Discussion

Across all MFIs countrywide, membership growth has been positive since 2011, though it seems to have generally slowed in pace after 2015/16. Disbursements steadily increased until 2018/19 but then dipped. We observe this from our surveyed branches as well: total disbursements, for all surveyed MFIs and the major three MFIs, show a declining trend in 2019/20, but then rise in 2020/21. Net savings, however, have maintained their countrywide rising trend since 2012. Disbursements were primarily in agriculture and trade and business activities over the decade. The major three MFIs—in terms of our baseline census respondents' participation in surveyed villages—are still GB, BRAC, and ASA. GB has the highest membership on average. From the survey it is observed that female borrowers predictably have substantially higher savings. We also observe that average savings in some districts declined during the COVID-19 pandemic; this is similar in case of both forced savings and voluntary savings. The Rangpur district branches saw the largest decline in female savings in this context. Though relatively higher MFI branches reported to accept payments through MFS, only four branches reported disbursing through MFS. Given the incredible potential for technology in increasing loans and reducing costs, MFIs would greatly benefit from adopting digital financial services.

5. Microenterprise Access to Financial Services

Why and How Finance Matters for Microenterprise

Access to finance matters to running a business activity. Since there is a lag between production and revenue (profit) accrued by the enterprises, an enterprise needs running capital to meet the demand for buying raw materials and hiring labor to run the activity. Often entrepreneurs meet such costs using their own funds, which is inefficient and often inadequate to meet the demand; therefore, enhanced access to financial services at an affordable cost and in a timely manner offered by institutions such as banks is more desirable for an efficient allocation of resources. Moreover, as microenterprises provide both income and employment for a large percentage of rural households who cannot find enough employment in the farming sector, enhancing employment opportunities via increased access to affordable finance should be an enduring policy of any government. Access to finance does not mean only access to a financial outfit for borrowing; it also means access where they can save, remit money, pay bills, and insure their business activities. This is what a broader definition of financial inclusion means in the literature—households and enterprises must have access to an array of financial services (Khandker 2021, World Bank 2012).

There are two broad categories of finance available to microenterprises. Institutions such as banks and MFIs have been providing important financial services over the years. But one limitation is that customers must have access to branches of these institutions in order to access their services. The other form of financial services recently being provided is through MFS, which provide services via mobile phone technology, for example, and are therefore easily accessible to an entrepreneur. This makes it much easier for a micro or small entrepreneur to undertake cashless transactions and reach their destinations within minutes. However, MFS has limitations—it has not yet reached out to lend money for income-earning activities like MFIs or banks provide. Nevertheless, both categories of financial services are an integral part of finance and may serve the needs of microenterprises such as borrowing from MFIs and transferring money using MFS.

With this premise for needs of alternative sources of financial services, we examine now whether and what sources of financial services are accessed by microenterprises surveyed in our study.

Microenterprise Access to Alternative Sources of Institutional Finance

We define access in two ways—having an account with an institution and whether enterprises managed to borrow from and save with these institutions.[5] **Table 33** presents the distribution of microenterprises by access (having an account) of alternative sources of institutional financial services. Overall, some 20% of enterprises have an

---

[5] For brevity, we also include informal finance as part of finance. Although informal lenders charge exorbitant interest rates, they are able to provide loans sometimes easily on short notice; hence, they can be used to meet the short-term needs of an enterprise. However, for long-term needs for investment and other purposes, there is no alternative to institutional sources of finance such as banks.

account with banks, with the highest numbers registered for manufacturing (30%), followed by businesses (23%) and services (14.5%). On the other hand, some 71% of all enterprises have an account with an MFI, with the largest for services (76%) followed by businesses (69%) and manufacturing (66%). The sector distribution of this access is as follows: the largest share of MFI accounts is for services (76%), followed by businesses (69%) and manufacturing (66%). MFIs such as ASA, BRAC, and GB are the largest providers of microfinance, serving more than 75% of all account holders in the MSME sector. The overall rate of access to financial services when banks are included is as high as 79% for MSMEs, with the highest share for the service sector (81%), followed by businesses (78%) and manufacturing (74%).

Table 33: Access of MSME Households to Alternate Sources of Finance by Sector

Source of Finance	Manufacturing	Business	Services	All Sectors
Banks (%)	30.1	23.3	14.5	19.8
MFIs				
GB (%)	25.2	21.8	26.1	23.8
BRAC (%)	18.0	20.3	19.2	19.7
ASA (%)	26.8	27.7	35.5	31.0
Other MFIs (%)	20.5	25.6	21.4	23.6
Any MFI	65.5	68.5	75.6	71.4
Access to any source (banks or MFIs) (%)	74.3	77.6	80.6	78.7
N	45	452	391	888

GB = Grameen Bank; MFI = microfinance institution; MSME = micro, small, and medium-sized enterprise.

Source: Authors' calculations based on the ADB–BIDS Digital Microcredit Survey 2021.

Another way to measure financial inclusion for MSME is by the amount of loans microenterprises owe to either a bank or an MFI. **Table 34** presents the incidence of borrowing and **Table 35** shows the distribution of enterprises by the amount of loans outstanding with an institution. As per the·extent of borrowing, the share of MSMEs with an outstanding loan with a bank is only 5%–7% for manufacturing, 6% for businesses, and only 3% for services. In contrast, 59% of microenterprises borrowed from MFIs, with ASA having the largest share (26%), followed by 19% from GB, 13% from BRAC, and 18% from all other MFIs. Similarly, the incidence of borrowing is 47% for manufacturing, 58% for businesses, and 62% for services. The incidence of borrowing from informal sources is about 6% for MSMEs, with 9% for business, 6% for manufacturing, and only 3% for services. Therefore, the largest lenders, among all categories of finance—formal and informal together—are MFIs, not banks.

Table 34: Incidence of Borrowing of MSME Households from Alternate Sources by Sector
(%)

Source of Outstanding Loans	Manufacturing	Business	Services	All Sectors
Banks	7.0	6.3	3.3	5.0
MFIs				
GB	19.3	17.0	20.8	18.8
BRAC	5.0	15.9	10.7	13.1
ASA	20.9	23.8	29.0	25.9
Other MFIs	14.6	19.1	16.7	17.9
Any MFI	47.1	58.2	61.7	59.2
Informal moneylenders	5.9	8.9	3.4	6.4
N	45	452	391	888

GB = Grameen Bank; MFI = microfinance institution; MSME = micro, small, and medium-sized enterprise.

Source: Authors' calculations based on the ADB–BIDS Digital Microcredit Survey 2021.

This is also evident from Table 35, which presents the distribution of microenterprises' loans outstanding from alternative sources of finance. Thus, the average amount of loans outstanding of the MSME sector as a whole are Tk20,546 from MFIs, compared with only Tk7,166 from banks and Tk4,114 from informal lenders. The largest amount of loans outstanding by sector are in manufacturing (Tk26,712), followed by businesses (Tk22,432) and services (Tk17,566). Thus, MSME loans outstanding from MFIs are disproportionately higher for the manufacturing sector compared with other sectors. This is also the case with banks and informal lenders.

Table 35: Outstanding Loans of MSME Households from Alternate Sources by Sector
(Tk)

Source of Outstanding Loans	Manufacturing	Business	Services	All Sectors
Banks	25,143.8	9,328.4	2,532.3	7,169.5
MFIs				
GB	2,806.9	3,706.6	4,006.6	3,792.2
BRAC	3,277.3	4,819.5	2,822.9	3,886.4
ASA	7,950.2	5,613.1	7,212.6	6,413.8
Other MFIs	12,678.0	8,292.9	3,523.8	6,453.8
All MFIs	26,712.4	22,432.1	17,565.9	20,546.2
Informal moneylenders	7,889.9	6,741.7	503.1	4,114.3
N	45	452	391	888

GB = Grameen Bank; MFI = microfinance institution; MSME = micro, small, and medium-sized enterprise.

Source: Authors' calculations based on the ADB–BIDS Digital Microcredit Survey 2021.

Microenterprise Access to Mobile Financial Services

MFS has been emerging as a major type of financial services accessed by rural households in recent years. MFS does not extend any loan to their customers, nor does any institutional financial agency extend any loan for income-generating activities using mobile technology.[6] There are three major MFS providers active in Bangladesh. The bKash, established in 2011, is the largest MFS, accounting more than 70% of all accounts in Bangladesh (Murshid et al. 2020). However, it is not known what the percentage of MSMEs based in rural areas have an account with bKash and other MFS providers. Like households, microenterprises are likely to access mobile financial services for different purposes such as paying money to purchase raw materials, receiving money from customers for products and services, paying electric bills or repaying loans to lenders, and depositing money as savings with an institutional financial agency.

Table 36 presents the distribution of microenterprises by whether or not they have an account with MFS. As high as 79% of microenterprises seem to have an account with MFS. The bKash alone accounts for 48% of MFS accounts. While Nagad alone accounts for only 5% of microenterprise accounts, Rocket has less than 1% of such accounts. However, 25% of microenterprises have an account with multiple MFS. The distribution of bKash accounts, the largest provider of mobile finance, is similar for each of the three microenterprise sectors.[7] Thus, manufacturing accounts for 50% of bKash accounts, followed by businesses (49%) and services (46%). Data clearly show that rural microenterprises rely heavily on mobile finance for day-to-day transactions for different purposes.

---

[6]   A bKash, together with a commercial bank, City Bank, has introduced a short-term loan (3 months) to its customers using its electronic know-your-customer database. This was introduced all over the country on 14 December 2021, right after our survey was completed.

[7]   A microenterprise can carry out a transaction through MFS without having an account with MFS. This table considers both MFS account holders and no account holders who undertake transactions of any type over the last month.

Table 36: Access of MSME Households to Alternate Mobile Financial Services Providers by Sector
(%)

MFS providers	Manufacturing	Business	Services	All Sectors
bKash only (%)	50.2	48.8	46.3	47.8
Nagad only (%)	0.3	2.8	7.8	4.8
Rocket only (%)	0	0.3	0.7	0.4
Multiple providers (%)	23.3	27.1	22.4	24.9
Any providers (%)	73.9	79.4	78.1	78.5
N	45	452	391	888

MFS = mobile financial services, MSME = micro, small, and medium-sized enterprise.

Source: Authors' calculations based on the ADB–BIDS Digital Microcredit Survey 2021.

Table 37 shows the distribution of microenterprise transactions of MFS by frequency and purpose. It shows that as much as 76% of all microenterprises carried out some type of transactions over the last month, with the highest for services (78%), followed by businesses (75%) and manufacturing (62%). On average, enterprises carried out two transactions each month. The average monthly amount of money received by microenterprise was Tk2,698 compared with Tk1,675 being spent. That is, they received about 60% more than what they sent out. Only about 1% of microenterprises used MFS for any type of transaction for microfinance operations, showing that they are hardly digitalized.[8]

Table 37: Frequency and Amount of Mobile Financial Services Transactions by MSME Households by Sector in the Last 30 Days

MFS transaction features	Manufacturing	Business	Services	All Sectors
Share of households using MFS transactions (%)	62.4	75.0	78.0	75.7
Frequency of MFS transactions	3.7	2.8	1.1	2.1
Amount of money received (Tk)	5,618.3	3,706.4	1,145.9	2,697.6
Amount of money sent (Tk)	1,464.0	2,767.0	372.8	1,674.5
Share of households using MFS for microcredit transactions (%)	0	1.2	1.0	1.1
N	45	452	391	888

MFS = mobile financial services; MSME = micro, small, and medium-sized enterprise.

Source: Authors' calculations based on the ADB–BIDS Digital Microcredit Survey 2021.

Determinants of Microenterprise Access to Alternative Sources of Institutional and Mobile Finance

Now we examine the supply- and demand-side factors affecting a household's participation in institutional finance such as MFIs and mobile finance. Participation in any type of finance is an outcome determined by demand-side factors such as owners' characteristics (age, education, and gender), and local market characteristics such as community-level wages and prices, while supply-side factors include variables such as whether the village has a mobile finance agency or an MFI office, as well as the interest rates charged by the institutions. However, as

---

[8]   Only nine enterprises carried out an MFS operation for microfinance transaction. These enterprises borrow money from BRAC, an agency that recently introduced digital transaction of microfinance operation such as paying off loan or receiving loan amount, and deposit money for savings. This small percentage implies digitalization of microfinance even in such a minimal sense—because lending is not digitalized yet—is very limited.

interest rates charged by MFIs do not vary across villages, nor does the service charge for mobile financial services across villages, they are not included in the participation equation.

Consider the following participation for either MFI or MFS or both, given that a household belongs to an MSME group as follows:

$$Y_{ij} = \alpha + \beta X_{ij} + \gamma V_j + \delta F_j + \varepsilon_{ij} \tag{1}$$

where Y_{ij} represents participation in MFI, MFS, or both of i-th household engaged in an enterprise located in j-th village; X_{ij} represents vector of household characteristics of i-th enterprise based in j-th village; V_j represents village-level characteristics such as whether village has a market and a paved road that are exogenously given to the functioning of an enterprise; F_j indicates the vector of finance-specific factors such as whether the financial service is available in the village; and ε_{ij} are identically and independently distributed errors. α, β, γ, and δ are unknown coefficients to be estimated.

Estimation of participation equation (1) for a household running a microenterprise activity is not independent of why certain households participate in an MSME activity in the first place. This means adoption of microenterprise activity as an income- and employment-generating activity must be accounted for before estimating an enterprise's participation in mobile finance or microfinance. Consider the following adoption equation of a household engaged in MSME:

$$E_{ij} = \pi_0 + \pi_1 X_{ij} + \pi_1 V_j + \pi_2 F_j + u_{ij} \tag{2}$$

where E_{ij} indicates a household's participation in MSME activity of any type. All other variables are the same as before. The π's are unknown parameters to be estimated, and u_{ij} are identically and independently distributed errors.

This means the estimation of equation (1) cannot be independent of equation (2) as errors of both equations are correlated. Thus, the unobserved heterogeneity affecting MSME adoption also affects participation in mobile finance or microfinance. This suggests that endogeneity needs to be taken care of before we can estimate equation (1) successfully. The standard method for correcting for such joint distribution of errors is a two-stage switching regression (Maddala 1983). Based on the first-stage equation of MSME adoption (equation 2), we can have two versions of equation (1):

$$Y_{1ij} = \alpha + \beta X_{1ij} + \gamma V_{1j} + \delta F_{1j} + \varepsilon_{1ij} \qquad \textbf{(1a)} \quad \text{if household adopts MSME activities; and}$$

$$Y_{0ij} = \alpha + \beta X_{0ij} + \gamma V_{0j} + \delta F_{0j} + \varepsilon_{0ij} \qquad \textbf{(1b)} \quad \text{if household does not adopt MSME activities.}$$

The error terms, u_i, ε_1 and ε_0, are assumed to have a tri-variate normal distribution with mean vector zero and covariance matrix:

$$\Omega = \begin{bmatrix} \sigma_1^2 & \sigma_{01} & \sigma_{1u} \\ & \sigma_0^2 & \sigma_{0u} \\ & & \sigma_u^2 \end{bmatrix}$$

where, σ_u^2, σ_1^2, and σ_0^2 are the variances of u_i, ε_1, and ε_0 respectively; and σ_{1u}, σ_{0u}, and σ_0 are covariances of ε_1 and u_i, ε_0 and u_i, and ε_0 and ε_1, respectively. In a switching regression model, equations (1a) and (1b) are run after controlling for a household's selection bias in adopting MSME activities.

The first-stage regression of equation (2) presented in **Table 38** shows that adoption of an enterprise activity is not exogenously fixed. Rather it is influenced by an array of factors both at the individual, household, and village level. A household headed by a male is more likely (by more than 15 percentage points) to participate in such an activity. Both the age and education of the household head matter—younger heads and heads with secondary education are more likely to engage in microenterprise activities. Households with a larger number of adult female members are more likely to be involved in such nonfarm activities. Landholding decreases microenterprise participation while nonland asset increases it. A 10% increase in land assets reduces participation by 0.2 percentage point, while a 10% increase in nonland asset increases household microenterprise participation by 0.5 percentage point. Households with grid electricity are more likely to participate, indicating a wealth effect. Microenterprise participation is also higher in villages with access to MFIs. The closer the village is to a district town, the more likely a household will participate in a microenterprise activity, indicating a backward linkage between urban and rural activities.

Table 38: Determinants of Household Adoption of MSME Activities—Probit Estimates

Explanatory Variables	Marginal Effects	Means of Explanatory Variables
HH head is male (Male=1, Female=0)	0.149**	94.3
	(2.77)	(0.233)
Age of head (years)	-0.002*	45.3
	(-1.85)	(12.3)
Head completed primary level of education	0.024	0.285
	(0.89)	(0.451)
Head completed secondary level of education	0.103*	0.075
	(1.89)	(0.263)
Head completed post-secondary level of education	-0.014	0.076
	(-0.27)	(0.264)
No. adult males (age>=18) in HH	-0.006	1.387
	(-0.36)	(0.729)
No. adult females (age>=18) in HH	0.047**	1.376
	(2.53)	(0.638)
Log HH agricultural land (decimals)	-0.017**	1.498
	(-2.74)	(2.042)
Log HH non-land asset (Tk)	0.051**	11.383
	(4.56)	(1.196)
HH has grid electricity	0.086*	0.901
	(1.91)	(0.299)
Village has secondary school	-0.004	0.454
	(-0.17)	(0.498)
Village has paved roads	0.035	0.767
	(1.00)	(0.423)
Village has health centers	-0.013	0.545
	(-0.44)	(0.498)
Village has banks	-0.046	0.101
	(-0.97)	(0.301)
Village has markets	0.006	0.645
	(0.19)	(0.479)

continued on next page

Table 38 continued

Explanatory Variables	Marginal Effects	Means of Explanatory Variables
Village MFIs	0.079*	0.174
	(1.86)	(0.379)
Village has agricultural extension program	–0.023	0.220
	(–0.66)	(0.414)
Village has MFS	–0.038	0.760
	(–1.13)	(0.427)
Village distance to district (km)	–0.002**	26.3
	(–2.24)	(17.6)
Village distance to upazilla (km)	–0.0002	8.9
	(–0.10)	(5.8)
Wald χ^2	326.41	–
p> χ^2	0.0000	–
Pseudo R^2	0.067	–
N	2,993	

HH = household; km = kilometer; MFI = microfinance institution; MFS = mobile financial services; MSME = micro, small, and medium-sized enterprise.

Notes: Explanatory variables also include village-level prices of consumer goods. * and ** refer to statistical significance at 10% and 5%, respectively. Figures in parentheses are t-statistics (based on robust standard errors clustered at village-level) in the marginal effects column and standard deviation in the mean column.

Source: Authors' calculations based on the ADB–BIDS Digital Microcredit Survey 2021.

Given the estimates of an adoption function of equation (2), the second-stage regression of equations (1a and 1b), as represented by a participation function in either financial services (microfinance or mobile finance) or in both categories of services, is estimated for both types of households—households engaged in microenterprise and households not engaged in microenterprises. Note that both types of households are recipients of microfinance of mobile finance services. Hence, it is possible to estimate equation (2) for both groups of households. The role of endogeneity of microenterprise adoption in either equation of MFI or MFS participation is measured by the coefficient of the inverse Mills ratio (λ), which is the ratio of normal density function to cumulative density function of E. The inclusion of inverse Mills ratio in the second-stage equation controls for endogeneity of MSME adoption. If the coefficients of Mills' ratio are statistically significant it follows that joint distribution of errors of equations (1) and (2) are highly correlated, meaning participation in MFS or MFI is not independent of MSME adoption.

As **Table 39** shows, this is the case for MFS or MFI participation, especially for those who participated in financial services but not in microenterprises.

Table 39: Determinants of Household Adoption of Microfinance Institution and Mobile Financial Services after Sample Selection for MSME Adoption Is Corrected—Two-Stage Probit Estimates

Explanatory Variables	MFI adoption		MFS adoption		Adoption of both MFI and MFS	
	MSME HHs	Non-MSME HHs	MSME HHs	Non-MSME HHs	MSME HHs	Non-MSME HHs
HH head is male (Male = 1, Female = 0)	–0.266	0.497**	–0.213	0.237*	–0.404	0.382**
	(–1.35)	(4.28)	(–1.21)	(1.94)	(–0.92)	(4.04)
Age of head (years)	0.007	–0.009**	0.004	–0.006	0.005	–0.008**
	(1.18)	(–4.98)	(0.82)	(–3.42)	(0.65)	(–4.54)

continued on next page

Table 39 continued

Explanatory Variables	MFI adoption		MFS adoption		Adoption of both MFI and MFS	
	MSME HHs	Non-MSME HHs	MSME HHs	Non-MSME HHs	MSME HHs	Non-MSME HHs
Head completed primary level of education	-0.186** (-2.07)	0.012 (0.29)	-0.043 (-0.64)	0.084** (2.17)	-0.147 (-1.57)	0.064* (1.64)
Head completed secondary level of education	-0.650** (-2.09)	0.088 (0.84)	-0.297 (-1.12)	0.140 (1.61)	-0.449 (-1.50)	0.098 (0.95)
Head completed post-secondary level of education	-0.146 (-1.56)	-0.288** (-4.64)	0.104* (1.65)	0.034 (0.56)	-0.040 (-0.37)	-0.241** (-4.35)
No. adult males (age> =18) in HH	0.009 (0.27)	0.049* (1.66)	0.101** (3.07)	0.037 (1.53)	0.071* (1. 91)	0.037 (1.43)
No. adult females (age> =18) in HH	-0.174 (-1.25)	0.144** (2.95)	-0.097 (-1.01)	0.192** (4.49)	-0.121 (-0.74)	0.195** (4.14)
Log HH agricultural land (decimals)	0.043 (0.85)	-0.083** (-4.76)	0.049 (1.34)	-1.032** (-2.28)	0.039 (0.66)	-0.067** (-4.01)
Log HH non-land asset (Tk)	-0.152 (-1.00)	0.154** (3.33)	-0.094 (-0.87)	0.137** (3.75)	-0.116 (-0.67)	0.160** (3.46)
HH has grid electricity	-0.260* (-1.63)	0.333** (4.14)	-0.254** (-3.33)	-0.112* (-1.75)	-0.443 (-1.98)	0.150* (1.85)
Village has secondary school	0.033 (0.57)	0.010 (0.25)	-0.011 (-0.26)	-0.088** (-2.60)	-0.014 - (0.23)	-0.067* (-1.83)
Village has paved roads	-0.208** (-2.01)	0.096 (1.49)	-0.083 (-0.96)	0.101* (1.73)	-0.136 (-0.99)	0.080 (1.34)
Village has health centers	0.075 (1.20)	-0.073* (-1.73)	0.088* (1.91)	-0.014 (-0.37)	0.105* (1.63)	-0.020 (-0.46)
Village has banks	0.162 (1.20)	-0.335** (-5.41)	0.176** (2.12)	-0.084 (-1.21)	0.190 (1.12)	-0.067** (-2.62)
Village MFIs	-0.446 (-1.55)	0.310** (4.07)	-0.207 (-1.09)	0.116** (2.02)	-0.243 (-0.89)	0.258** (2.99)
Village has agricultural extension program	0.200 (1.93)	-0.018 (-0.35)	-0.019 (-0.23)	-0.033 (-0.67)	0.119 (0.87)	-0.032 (-0.62)
Village has MFS	0.202* (1.68)	-0.069 (-1.20)	0.046 (0.53)	-0.042 (-0.93)	0.087 (0.69)	-0.056 (-1.06)
Village distance to district (km)	0.009 (1.30)	-0.007** (-2.89)	0.005 (1.01)	-0.004 (-2.25)	0.008 (1.05)	-0.007 (-2.77)
Village distance to upazilla (km)	-0.007* (-0.91)	-0.008** (-2.56)	0.009** (2.47)	-0.002 (-0.51)	-0.001 (-0.34)	-0.006 (-1.74)
Inverse Mills Ratio (λ)	-2.038 (-1.41)	1.624** (2.60)	-1.457* (-1.78)	1.278** (2.51)	-1.740 (-1.04)	1.667** (2.68)
Wald χ^2	241.1	464.04	217.52	355.01	292.04	386.94
p> χ^2	0.000	0.000	0.000	0.000	0.000	0.000
Pseudo R^2	0.146	0.130	0.167	0.152	0.134	0.117
N	934	2,059	934	2,059	934	2,059

HH = household; km = kilometer; MFI = microfinance institution; MFS = mobile financial services; MSME = micro, small, and medium-sized enterprise.

Notes: Explanatory variables also include village-level prices of consumer goods. * and ** refer to statistical significance of 10% and 5%, respectively. Figures in parentheses are t-statistics (based on robust standard errors clustered at village-level).

Source: Authors' calculations based on the ADB–BIDS Digital Microcredit Survey 2021.

A household headed by a man is more likely to participate in MFI, MFS, or both types of financial services who are not necessarily engaged in microenterprise activities. Similarly, younger heads of households are more likely to use financial services of either category if they are not engaged in MSME activities. Heads with primary education are less likely to participate in MFI activity, if they are members of MSME groups. In contrast, the non-MSME groups with primary education are more likely to use MFS or both MFI and MFS services. Similarly, non-MSME households headed by a post-secondary graduate are less likely to participate in financial services at the margin compared with their counterpart MSME households. The marginal reduction in participation is 28.8% for MFI and 24.1% for both MFI and MFS participation for this group. But MSME households headed by a post-secondary graduate are more likely to participate in MFS. It is about 10.4 percentage points higher at the margin for them compared with counterpart non-MSME households. Participation rates are higher for MSME households in the case of MFS (10 percentage points more) and both MFI and MFS (7 percentage points more) than non-MSME households if the number of adult males is higher in the family. However, participation with MFI is higher for non-MSME households with a higher number of adult male members. The same pattern holds for non-MSME households with a higher number of female members: 14% in the case of MFI, 19% in case of MFS, and 19.5% for both MFI and MFS.

At the margin, landholding reduces participation rates of non-MSME households in MFI, MFS, and both MFI and MFS at the margin compared with MSME households. The reverse is true for non-land asset holding (i.e., participation in MFI, MFS, and both type of financial services is higher among non-MSME households at the margin compared with MSME households). For households with electricity access, participation rates in MFI, MFS, or both are lower (higher) for MSME (non-MSME) households at the margin.

The probability of participation in MFS and both MFI and MFS is lower among non-MSME compared with MSME households in villages with a secondary school. Participation in MFI and MFS services is also sensitive to other village-level variables. Of particular interest are variables affecting participation and the availability of MFI and MFS services in the villages. Among non-MSME households, participation in MFI or MFS services or both is higher at the margin compared with MSME households. Thus, the participation rate among non-MSME households is about 31 percentage points higher for MFI, 12 percentage points higher for MFS, and 26 percentage points higher for both financial services than those for MSME households. In contrast, availability of MFS at the village level affects MSME household participation by as much as 20 percentage points. The distance to a district or *upazilla* (town) negatively affects the participation of MFI or MFS or both types of services, especially among those without MSME activities. This means, the closer the village to the district town, for example, the greater the participation of households in MFI or MFS. The results thus indicate that a variety of both demand- and supply-side factors affects a household's participation decision in mobile finance or microfinance services. This is true for both MSME and non-MSME households. Finally, a positive and statistically significant coefficient of the inverse Mills ratio in MFI participation for non-MSME households means that unobserved variables that increase MSME adoption also increase participation in MFI services. On the other hand, the relationship is opposite in the case of MFS for MSME households.

Discussion

Data analysis suggests that microenterprises have access to both MFIs and MFS, but not to banks. As much as 70% of microenterprises have an account with an MFS or MFI. This means microenterprises have good access to financial services. This, of course, does not mean their access is enough to meet the various needs of an enterprise running its operations smoothly and efficiently. Besides using MFS, for example, to remit or receive money for a variety of purposes, MSMEs also need a reliable source for borrowing and saving money. MFS are not yet that source. On the other hand, although MFIs are a source of borrowing, they charge interest rates as high as 24% for loans repayable within 1 year. As aggregate MFI statistics demonstrate (section 4), MFI borrowers repay their loan on time—loan recovery rates are as high as 95% among MFI branches. Yet, MSMEs do not have access to bank loans, a source that provides a large amount of loans per customer for a longer duration and at a much lower rate (i.e., as low as 9%).

6. Assessing the Impact of Financial Services on Microenterprise Productivity

We discussed microenterprise access to institutional financial services such as microfinance and MFS in section 5. We also examined the factors affecting a household's adoption of a microenterprise activity. This section discusses rates of return to capital investment in MSMEs to infer whether financing MSMEs through MFIs is worth supporting and whether such financing increases microenterprise productivity. By financial services, we mean not only access to institutional (such as banks and MFIs) but also MFS. Finance matters in raising productivity (measured by value of products produced by the enterprise per unit of capital, for example) in two ways—by (i) providing startup capital (fixed capital) and (ii) supporting production through financing working capital. If capital is an important source of productivity, then access to finance matters for raising productivity. It also follows that constraints to access to finance can hinder microenterprise productivity and growth.

Access to finance can be constrained to an enterprise for various economic and noneconomic reasons. For example, a lack of collateral can be an important factor constraining access when institutional access is based on a sufficient amount of physical collateral (e.g., landholding or nonland assets) being provided by the entrepreneurs. On the other hand, access to finance can be constrained by noneconomic factors such as distance to a branch of an institution providing financial services. Here, we examine MSME access to different types of financial services as well as categories of economic and noneconomic constraints hindering access to financial services. Thus, we also quantify the effect of improved access to finance on productivity. However, measuring the effects of access to finance on productivity involves a simultaneity bias in the sense that access to finance and an enterprise's productivity may be jointly determined by the same economic and noneconomic factors. It is often difficult to measure the precise effects of access to financial services on productivity without resolving this bias in estimation. This means estimates of productivity due to access to finance are likely to suffer from unobserved bias unless we resolve the endogeneity issue.

We discuss an econometric approach that helps resolve simultaneity bias due to endogeneity of access to financial services. We also estimate rates of return to investment in microenterprises to determine if investment in microenterprise growth is worth supporting. That is, we need to compare rates of return to capital employed in microenterprise and rates of interest in borrowing to justify if investment in MSME is worth the price of borrowing.

Salient Features of Microenterprise Activities

To understand how the MSME sector's productivity is determined and can further be enhanced to reduce rural poverty by increasing rural income and employment, it is important to discuss the salient features of the sector such as the sector distribution. As **Table 40** shows, business accounts for 52% of the sector, followed by services (43%) and manufacturing (only 4.8%). On the other hand, among the subsectors, manufacturing accounts for the highest share (7.5%) in Kurigram and the lowest in Dinajpur (3.3%). Among the districts, Dinajpur accounts for 25.8% of the MSME activities, followed by Rangpur (22%), Lalmonirhat (31.3%), Gaibandha (18.9%), and Kurigram (12.9%). Thus, business and services predominate the sector, accounting for 95% of MSME activities.

Table 40: Distribution of MSME Sectors by District
(%)

Sector	Dinajpur	Gaibandha	Kurigram	Lalmonirhat	Rangpur	All Districts
Manufacturing	3.3	3.8	7.5	6.0	4.9	4.8
Business	50.2	48.4	55.7	58.0	49.8	52.2
Services	46.5	47.8	36.8	36.0	45.3	43.0
All sectors	25.8	18.2	12.9	21.3	22.0	100.0
N	229	184	118	167	190	888

MSME = micro, small, and medium-sized enterprise.
Source: Authors' calculations based on the ADB–BIDS Digital Microcredit Survey 2021.

No wonder the sector is highly informal—only 27% of MSMEs are registered, with the highest share found in the manufacturing sector (49%), followed by services (29.5%) and business (23.6%) (**Table 41**). The informality of the sector is also represented by the location of the enterprise—while 58% of MSMEs are located adjacent to home, followed by 32% based on commercial locations and the rest (10%) based in other locations. Among the activities, manufacturing is by far the largest sector based in commercial locations (52%), compared with 37% in the case of business and 23% in the case of services.

Table 41: Salient Features of MSME by Sector

Feature	Manufacturing	Business	Services	All Sectors
Share of male owners or operators (%)	95.1	97.8	92.6	95.5
Operator or owner's age (years)	43.1	44.2	40.7	42.6
Operator or owner's education				
Below primary (%)	44.4	42.2	50.5	45.9
Primary (%)	29.4	33.7	31.1	32.3
Secondary (%)	16.9	13.3	8.7	11.5
Post-secondary (%)	9.3	10.8	9.7	10.3
Total workers	3.8	1.5	1.3	1.5
Share of hired labor (%)	55.3	16.3	16.8	21.5
MSME location				
Within dwelling or adjacent to dwelling (%)	34.4	54.8	64.3	57.9
Commercial locations (%)	52.3	36.9	22.8	31.6
Other locations (%)	13.3	8.2	12.9	10.5
Share of registered MSMEs (%)	49.1	23.6	29.5	27.3
MSME duration of operation (years)	11.3	9.2	8.0	8.8
MSME customers				
From same village (%)	44.8	64.5	43.0	54.7
From other rural areas (%)	64.1	68.5	78.7	72.6
From urban areas (%)	33.2	19.7	26.2	23.1
N	45	452	391	888

MSME = micro, small, and medium-sized enterprise.
Source: Authors' calculations based on the ADB–BIDS Digital Microcredit Survey 2021.

The average duration of enterprises' existence is higher for manufacturing (11 years), compared with 9 years for business and 8 years for services. The microenterprises serve the needs of the rural areas more than those of urban areas. For example, 55% to 70% of customers are located in rural areas compared with only 23% in urban towns.

The other features worth considering are the characteristics of owners, or who owns or runs these activities. More than 95% of MSMEs are owned by males, and the average age of owners is 43 years. Some 78% of owners have a primary or less than primary education. Some 22% of owners each have a secondary or post-secondary education. The average number of workers is less than two, and only 22% of workers are hired labor. However, manufacturing has the highest share of hired workers (55%), followed by 16% each in business and services.

Sources of Startup Capital of Microenterprises

Microenterprise activities are not only informal and largely based at home (hence, the term "cottage industries"), they are also established largely with their own finance. **Table 42** shows the distribution of sources of capital. We find that own sources (from assets and savings) account for more than 45% of the startup capital for all three categories of the MSME sector. The share is 56% in the case of services, followed by manufacturing (46%) and business (33%). While bank finance is miniscule, accounting for only 0.8% of the startup capital, MFIs account for 35% of startup capital overall, with the largest share for services (50.0%), followed by 28.9% for manufacturing and 23.4% for businesses. Like formal lenders, informal lenders contribute only about 1% to the startup capital of MSMEs.

Table 42: Distribution of the Source of Startup Capital of MSME by Sector
(%)

Source	Manufacturing	Business	Services	All Sectors
Own resources (assets, savings)	46.0	56.2	32.8	45.7
Loans from friends and relatives	6.6	11.1	9.8	10.4
Loans from MFIs	28.9	23.4	50.1	35.2
Loans from banks	0	1.4	0.1	0.8
Loans from informal sources	2.7	1.2	0.9	1.2
Other sources	15.8	6.6	5.2	6.4
N	45	452	391	888

MFI = microfinance institution; MSME = micro, small, and medium-sized enterprise.

Source: Authors' calculations based on the ADB–BIDS Digital Microcredit Survey 2021.

Rates of Return to Investment in Microenterprise Sector

Microenterprise contributes to household income and employment. To measure its role in rural income, it is important to determine the extent of income and productivity enjoyed by entrepreneurs. This assessment will also help estimate the rates of return to investment to justify whether further investment is profitable for the capital and time invested in this sector. This is important for both types of actors—those who depend on this sector for income and employment, and for those who are interested in supporting such activities by providing financial services (e.g., MFIs). It is also important for policymakers who design policies to support and enhance the sector's contribution to overall economic growth, as a large percentage of households are primarily engaged in this sector for income. All these considerations justify an analysis of profitability or rates of return to investment in this sector.

Income and cost data for MSMEs are important elements of enterprise-level surveys. Using such data, we will try to assess the growth potential of this sector by calculating its accounting profit. Table 43 presents the cost of microenterprise operations, revenue, and profit accrued by entrepreneurs. This is to determine which sector is most profitable among different sectors and by district. We also present the extent of working capital used and enterprise asset.

Table 43: MSME Inputs and Profitability by Sector

Inputs or Productivity Indicator	Manufacturing	Business	Services	All Sectors
Operating cost (Tk per year)	513,777.0	540,564.8	305,859.2	438,339.9
Family labor cost (imputed) (Tk per year)	232,265.3	212,173.8	177,659.6	198,301.6
Hired labor cost (Tk per year)	271,503.3	26,043.6	34,521.7	41,628.6
Working capital (Tk)	86,296.5	168,084.3	202,755.9	179,025.0
Enterprise asset (Tk)	384,307.4	261,045.4	204,307.3	242,588.8
Revenue (Tk per year)	617,568.2	791,153.6	685,462.0	737,320.4
Profit (not accounting for family labor) (Tk per year)	138,108.4	276,294.2	399,410.9	322,566.4
Profit (accounting for family labor) (Tk per year)	109,763.6	192,699.7	274,346.7	223,806.2
Profit margin (not accounting for family labor)	0.330	0.419	0.630	0.506
Profit margin (accounting for family labor)	0.276	0.277	0.392	0.326
Rate of return	0.233	0.449	0.674	0.531
N	45	452	391	888

MSME = micro, small, and medium-sized enterprise.

Note: Operating cost comprises all business expenses including cost of material, rent, fuel, hired labor, and other variable cost incurred by the enterprise. Family labor cost is imputed at the prevailing market wage rate. Profit margin is defined by the profit as a percentage of the revenue.

Source: Authors' calculations based on the ADB–BIDS Digital Microcredit Survey 2021.

The cost of an enterprise has two elements—operating cost and family labor cost. Operating cost includes the actual cost an enterprise incurs such as cost of materials, rent, hired labor, fuels, interest payments, cost of raw materials, and taxes. Family labor is often used at no cost, but since it has an opportunity cost, family labor needs to be imputed at the prevailing market wages. As Table 43 shows, hired labor cost is a very small percentage of operating cost, accounting for only 10% of the operating cost of the MSME sector as a whole. On the other hand, family labor cost imputed at market wage rates accounts for 45% of the operating cost of the MSME sector.

Profit is the revenue generated over the last 12 months less the operating cost. We created two measures of profit—one accounts for the family labor cost and the other does not. However, for all practical purposes, accounting for family labor is the most appropriate to determine if an investment is worth supporting such enterprises.[9] For comparison, we presented both measures of profit in Table 43. There are two important measures of profitability to determine the extent of profitability of investments in microenterprises. One such measure is the so-called profit margin, which is defined by the profit (taking account of the cost of family labor) as a percentage of the revenue.

---

[9]   Hence, this measure of profit that accounts for the opportunity cost of family labor is the appropriate measure as the true cost of the enterprise activity.

The other measure is the return on assets (ROA) to compare profitability among alternative investments in MSME and other areas of investment. The measure of ROA is defined commonly by the profit as percentage of enterprise assets.[10] There are alternative ways one can measure the assets of the enterprise to calculate the rate of return to assets. Following de Mel et al. (2008), we measure capital assets by combining the working capital and the value of the assets. We calculate the ROA by dividing profit (taking into account family labor cost) by the capital asset.

For comparisons of profitability of alternative microenterprise activities, we have presented both measures. The profit margin is an indicator of an enterprise's pricing strategies and how well it controls costs of operation. The profit margin measures how cost-effective an enterprise's performance is across sectors and as a whole. A higher profit margin indicates a high margin of economic safety. In contrast, the ROA is a productivity measure commonly used to determine how well the enterprise utilizes assets under command. It is also a measure that helps creditors and investors alike determine if lending or borrowing is worth the cost and whether an enterprise has repayment ability as compared with the opportunity cost of the capital.

As Table 43 shows, both the profit margin and rate of return are the highest for services and the lowest for manufacturing. That is, profit margin is 0.39 for services compared with 0.28 for both manufacturing and businesses. In contrast, the rate of return to assets is 67% for services, compared with 23% for manufacturing and 45% for businesses. The results indicate that the service sector is performing better than other activities. This is perhaps because the service sector requires lower operating costs compared with other sectors. The average ROA among MSMEs is 53%. The results seem higher but not entirely inconsistent with findings from other countries. For example, Zinman (2002) found the gross rates of return to capital in the United States in the order of 20%–58%. Banerjee and Duflo (2005) find the average rate of return to capital is 22% in India, while Caselli and Freyer (2007) observe the marginal rate to be 19% in Sri Lanka.

Estimated Rates of Return to Capital Using Production and Profit Functions

The above estimated rates of return are gross estimates of returns. They are influenced by enterprise, household, and community factors at both the demand for and supply of MSME products. To control the role of such factors, we resort to production and profit function approaches to estimate the ROA.

Consider the following Cobb–Douglas production function of MSME production:

$$Q_{ij} = A^{\alpha_0} K_{ij}^{\alpha} L_{ij}^{\beta} R_{ij}^{\gamma} \tag{3}$$

where Q_{ij} is the value of production of i-th enterprise located at j-th village, A is the measure of technology, K measures capital, L is labor, and R is other variable cost. To measure the rate of return to capital, labor and other variable cost, we estimate a logarithmic version of the above production function:

$$lnQ_{ij} = \alpha_0 lnA + \alpha lnK_{ij} + \beta lnL_{ij} + \gamma lnR_{ij} + \varepsilon_{ij} \tag{4}$$

---

[10]   Asset value is defined by the value of the building and other assets owned by the enterprise. It is often observed for the case of manufacturing units of MSMEs, but not observed for many businesses and services. Thus, the value of the enterprise is always undervalued and sometimes not reported. For those households that did not report any enterprise asset value, we impute a value of assets by regressing an asset function against a set of observed characteristics of enterprises for the subsample with observed asset values.

Here, α_0 measures the coefficient of technology; α measures the rate of return to capital; β measures the return to labor; and γ is the return to other costs, including raw materials.

Alternatively, we can estimate a profit function defined by the value of production less all variable costs, including costs of both family and hired labor. Here is the logarithmic function of Cobb–Douglas type of profit function as equation (4):

$$lnP_{ij} = \equiv \alpha_0 lnA + \alpha lnK_{ij} + \pi_{ij} \qquad (5)$$

where P_{ij} is a measure of profit.

Estimates of the production function and profit function of microenterprises are presented in **Table 44**. Both equations are estimated with good fitness. The R-squared is 0.41 for production function and 0.97 for profit function. That is, some 41% of variation in the production function is accounted for by the model, while 97% of variation in the profit function is accounted for by the profit function model. In both equations, the coefficient of the constant (α_0) measures technical growth, which is 3% as per the production function estimates and 9% as per the profit function estimates.

The most important estimates of both production and profit function considered are the net estimates of the ROA. As Table 44 shows, rate of return to capital according to production function is 38% compared with 22% as per the profit function estimates.

Table 44: Determinants of Productivity Using Production and Profit Function Approaches—Ordinary Least Squares Estimates

Explanatory Variables	Log revenue (Tk./year)	Log profit (Tk./year)
Log MSME capital (Tk)	0.377**	0.218**
	(5.49)	(2.99)
Log MSME labor cost (Tk/year)	0.193**	
	(2.54)	–
Log MSME other operating cost (Tk/year)	0.225**	
	(9.60)	–
Gender of MSME operator (Male = 1, Female = 0)	0.180	0.108
	(1.15)	(0.63)
Age of MSME operator (years)	–0.003	–0.009**
	(–0.96)	(–2.08)
MSME operator completed primary level of education	–0.048	–0.086*
	(–0.60)	(–0.95)
MSME operator completed secondary level of education	0.111	–0.461*
	(0.75)	(–1.71)
MSME operator completed post-secondary level of education	0.319**	–0.048
	(2.48)	(–0.27)
MSME activity is business	–0.132	0.286
	(–0.47)	(1.11)
MSME operator is services	–0.0002	0.303
	(–0.01)	(1.12)

continued on next page

Table 44 continued

Explanatory Variables	Log revenue (Tk./year)	Log profit (Tk./year)
MSME is household-based	0.176	0.478**
	(1.36)	(2.39)
MSME is operated in commercial location	0.260*	0.402**
	(1.84)	(2.01)
Village has secondary school	0.042	−0.262*
	(0.45)	(−1.83)
Village has health centers	−0.042	−0.024
	(−0.53)	(−0.20)
Village has banks	0.020	0.095
	(0.13)	(0.59)
Village has markets	0.132	0.410**
	(1.15)	(2.54)
Village MFIs	−0.119	0.018
	(−0.75)	(0.12)
Village has agricultural extension program	0.155**	0.169
	(2.01)	(1.57)
Village has MFS	0.063	−0.168
	(0.68)	(−1.24)
Village distance to district (km)	−0.004**	−0.004
	(−2.16)	(−1.48)
Village distance to pazila (km)	0.003	0.001
	(0.52)	(0.12)
Intercept	3.131**	9.101**
	(2.51)	(10.47)
R^2	0.406	0.966
N	888	888

MFI = microfinance institution; MFS = mobile financial services; MSME = micro, small, and medium-sized enterprise.

Notes: Explanatory variables also include village-level prices of consumer goods. * and ** refer to statistical significance of 10% and 5%, respectively. Figures in parentheses are t-statistics based on robust standard errors clustered at village-level.

Source: Authors' calculations based on the ADB–BIDS Digital Microcredit Survey 2021.

As mentioned earlier, the production function estimates are often subject to simultaneity bias because, although capital is fixed in the short run, other inputs in production such as use of labor and material and other associated costs (e.g., electricity bill), are jointly determined along with production. So, for the estimates of rate of return to capital, a profit function estimate is always preferred. Nonetheless, we present both estimates just for comparison and the results confirm that production function estimates are upper value of estimates of rates of return. However, we control for other factors, including enterprise-specific factors as well as village-level infrastructural factors, in both the production and profit function estimates. Therefore, the return estimates from production function estimates are most likely robust. We find the rate of return to labor is 19%, while it is 22.5% for other factors of production.

Among other important factors determining profit, the type of industry (whether business or manufacturing or services) does not matter, while location of industry matters. Thus, returns to location are 46% higher when the enterprise is based in a home and 40% higher when the enterprise is based in a commercial location compared with other places. While returns to profit are lower in a village with a secondary school and a paved road, returns are higher in villages with a market and agricultural extensions. However, the presence of an MFI branch office or MFS agents in a village does not yield any specific return to profit.

Rates of Return by Sources of Financial Services Accessed by Microenterprises

Table 45 presents a summary of the distribution of microenterprises who have accessed different categories of finances (institutional—meaning banks and MFIs, and mobile). By access, we mean whether or not an enterprise has an account with a financial service provider.[11]

Table 45: Access to Finance of MSME Households by Sector
(%)

Financial Service Type	Manufacturing	Business	Services	All Sectors
MFI only	7.8	11.6	12.3	11.7
MFS only	12.8	15.6	11.7	13.8
Bank only	0.3	1.2	1.6	1.3
MFI and MFS, no bank	36.5	42.7	53.8	47.2
Either MFI or MFS, and bank	29.8	22.1	12.9	18.5
Overall access to MFI	65.5	68.5	75.6	71.4
Overall access to MFS	73.9	79.4	78.1	78.5
Overall access to bank	30.1	23.3	14.5	19.8
Access to any source	87.1	93.1	92.3	92.5
Access to no source	12.9	6.9	7.7	7.5
N	45	452	391	888

MFI = microfinance institution; MFS = mobile financial services; MSME = micro, small, and medium-sized enterprise.

Note: Households are considered to have access to MFS only if they have MFS accounts. That is, those who use MFS but do not have an account are not considered to have access to MFS.

Source: Authors' calculations based on the ADB–BIDS Digital Microcredit Survey 2021.

There are three major categories of financial service providers—banks, MFIs, and MFS. Very few microenterprises have access to bank finance. Only 1.3% of MSME owners have a bank-only account. In contrast, some 12% of enterprises have an account with an MFI-only and 14% have an MFS-only account. Many microenterprises may have an account with both an MFI and MFS—the data show that as much as 47% of microenterprises have an account with both types of financial services. On the other hand, only 18.5% of enterprises have an account with a bank and an MFI or MFS. The overall access is about 71% for MFIs, compared with 79% for MFS and only 20% for banks. An overwhelming 93% of microenterprises have access to some type of financial service. This access rate is similar for all three categories of microenterprises—87% for manufacturing, 93% for business, and 92% for services.

What does this mean to enterprises in terms of rates of return measured by the observed profit margin and returns to capital? **Table 46** presents the distribution of MSMEs by the level of productivity and rates of return to investment by categories of financial services accessed by microenterprises.

---

[11]   That means, those who carried out any transaction via MFS without having an account are not included with MFI only (46%).

Table 46: MSME Productivity by Access to Finance

Productivity Indicator	MFI Only	MFS Only	MFI and MFS, No Bank	Either MFS or MFI, and Bank	Access to Any Source	Access to No Source
Revenue (Tk per year)	616,329.6	778,143.3	621,532.1	1,171,008.0	761,352.5	440,762.9
Profit (Tk per year)	257,439.0	411,838.9	320,363.7	293,756.2	328,774.2	245,961.4
Profit margin	0.504	0.530	0.5444	0.345	0.499	0.583
Rate of return	0.459	0.676	0.581	0.375	0.543	0.358
N	117	129	413	157	823	65

MFI = microfinance institution; MFS = mobile financial services; MSME = micro, small, and medium-sized enterprise.

Note: Figures for bank-only access are not reported as the sample is too low to be reliable.

Source: Authors' calculations based on the ADB–BIDS Digital Microcredit Survey 2021.

Overall, the profit margin (the measure of cost-effectiveness of an enterprise) is higher for those who do not have an account with any type of financial services (58%), compared with only 50% for those who have an account with any source of finance. That is, profit is some 58% of revenue for the former group compared with 50% of revenue for the latter group. One can infer also that those who do have an account with any type of financial agency are perhaps better managed than those who do not have an account.[12] However, the average rate of return to capital is much higher for those that accessed any financial services (54%) compared with those who did not have such an account (36%). Thus, the average rate of return to capital is highest (68%) for microenterprises that have an account with an MFS, followed by those who have an account with both an MFI and MFS (58%) and for those with any account with an MFI only (46%). This means the profitability and rate of return of enterprises are likely to be related to access to microfinance and mobile finance.

Rates of Return by Extent of Credit Constraint

Also, if access is measured by whether an enterprise borrows from a financial institution such as an MFI, then one can see if the performances of an enterprise vary by whether an enterprise is credit constrained or not. **Table 47** shows the distribution of households (MSME, non-MSME, and all types) by degree of credit constraint. A household is credit-constrained when it does not receive the amount of borrowing against what it asks for. Accordingly, about 5% of households are found to be credit-constrained, with the highest share among sectors being those households engaged in manufacturing (about 7%). Another measure of credit constraints is the credit gap ratio, which is the ratio of the credit gap (difference between credit demanded and credit received) to credit demanded. As we can see from Table 47, the credit gap ratio does not vary across sectors, and it averages 1.3% for all MSME households. Non-MSME households have a slightly higher credit gap ratio (1.6%). Overall, the credit gap ratio is 1.5% for all loans.

---

[12]   This difference may not be significant or subject to small sample bias as there are only 7.5% of 888 microenterprises (only 66 enterprises) in the latter group.

Table 47: Credit Constraints for Microcredit Loans

Indicator of Credit Constraints	MSME Households				Non-MSME Households	All Households
	Manufacturing	Business	Services	All Sectors		
Incidence of credit constraints (%)	8.7	4.1	4.6	5.0	5.6	5.4
Credit gap ratio (%)	1.2	1.3	1.2	1.3	1.6	1.5
N	73	700	631	1,601	2,267	3,868

MSME = micro, small, and medium-sized enterprise.

Note: Credit gap ratio is the ratio of the credit gap (difference between credit demanded and credit received) to credit demanded.

Source: Authors' calculations based on the ADB–BIDS Digital Microcredit Survey 2021.

Table 48 presents the distribution of profitability for credit-constrained and non-credit-constrained microenterprises. Enterprises were asked if they were credit-constrained from the supply side (or providers of credit).

Table 48: Productivity by Credit Constraint of MSME Households by Sector

Productivity Indicator	Manufacturing (Credit-constrained HHs=17.5%)		Business (Credit-constrained HHs=8.6%)		Services (Credit-constrained HHs=10.0%)		All MSME Households (Credit-constrained HHs=9.6%)	
	Not credit-constrained	Credit-constrained	Not credit-constrained	Credit-constrained	Not credit-constrained	Credit-constrained	Not credit-constrained	
Revenue (Tk per year)	702,236.7	476,356.7	697,291.9	665,826.0	685,342.6	547,762.6	692,042.4
Profit (Tk per year)	204,393.3	203,717.3	265,173.3	305,554.8	376,019.0	243,889.2	313,279.5
Profit margin	0.391	0.487	0.429	0.528	0.604	0.498	0.508
Rate of return	0.411	0.468	0.360	0.514	0.614	0.446	0.534
N	24	24	273	25	247	53	544

HH = household; MSME = micro, small, and medium-sized enterprise.

Source: Authors' calculations based on the ADB–BIDS Digital Microcredit Survey 2021.

Based on such information, we present differential performances of enterprises by whether enterprises were credit-constrained or not. On average, rates of return are higher for non-credit-constrained enterprises than for credit-constrained. Thus, the rate of return to capital is 45% for credit-constrained enterprises compared with 53% for non-credit-constrained enterprises. This means, better access to institutional finance can be a way to enhance the productivity of MSMEs. The findings are a priori consistent with theory. In theory, if returns to capital are diminishing (according to the law of diminishing returns), constrained entrepreneurs are likely stuck with lower returns because of the lack of access to sufficient capital. That is, it is possible that returns are lower for credit-constrained than for non-credit-constrained enterprises. While this is true for microenterprises engaged in the service sector, this is not true for businesses. That is, rates of return to investment are higher (47%) for credit-constrained businesses compared with only 36% for non-credit-constrained enterprises. In any case, overall better credit access matters for raising an enterprise's productivity.

Does Better Access to Financial Services Matter in an Enterprise's Productivity?

We would like to pursue a direct estimate of the return to better access to a credit facility such as MFIs—we consider only MFIs because they represent the largest and perhaps the only financing facility for many MSME—using a production or a profit function approach where MFI account is an additional variable. However, we also interact MFI with MFS to see if digitalization of microfinance activities (at least for loan repayment or savings deposit through MFS) matters as an additional role in raising enterprise productivity. In other words, we estimate the Cobb–Douglas specification of production function (4) and profit function (5) with MFIs directly and the interaction of MFIs and MFS as additional variables.

In our equation, "MFI" measures whether the enterprise has an account and the interaction term "MFI*MFS" measures an interaction of having both MFI and MFS accounts. However, as we saw in section 5, both participations in MFI and MFS activities are endogenously determined by the same factors that affect MSME production and productivity directly. Hence, instead of directly using the participation dummies (e.g., whether having an account with MFI or not), we use both the predicted values of MFI or joint participation of MFI and MFS based on the estimates reported in section 5.

Table 49 presents the results. We find that the digitalization of microfinance (measured by the interaction dummy of MFI and MFS) does not mean much in raising MSME productivity. However, MFI access (measured by an account) improved MSME production by 4.2% annually and profit by 2.6%. That is, improved access to finance has an average return of 4.2% to microenterprise income every year above and beyond what is accounted for by capital and other factors. However, finding no significant impact of MFS in conjunction with MFI participation is not surprising, given that MFS are used primarily for cash transfers such as paying off the cost of raw materials or remitting money using a mobile account (e.g., bKash), and not used as an outlet for accessing microfinance services.

Table 49: Impacts of Microfinance and Mobile Financial Services on Production and Profit of MSME Activities—Two-Stage Estimation

Explanatory Variables	Log revenue (Tk/year)	Log profit (Tk/year)
Household participates in microfinance	0.042** (2.20)	0.026 (1.17)
Household participates in microfinance X Household has MFS account	−0.022 (−1.60)	−0.014 (−0.87)
Gender of MSME operator (Male=1, Female=0)	0.134 (0.80)	0.171 (0.91)
Age of MSME operator (years)	−0.002 (−0.75)	−0.008** (−2.04)
MSME operator completed primary level of education	−0.056 (−0.70)	−0.067 (−0.76)
MSME operator completed secondary level of education	0.105 (0.65)	−0.554** (−2.04)

continued on next page

Table 49 continued

Explanatory Variables	Log revenue (Tk/year)	Log profit (Tk/year)
MSME operator completed post-secondary level of education	0.281*** (2.27)	-0.086 (-0.54)
MSME activity is business	-0.125 (-0.44)	0.286 (1.11)
MSME operator is services	0.002 (0.01)	0.271 (0.92)
MSME is household-based	0.203* (1.67)	0.496*** (2.68)
MSME is operated in commercial location	0.289** (2.18)	0.394** (2.14)
Log MSME capital (Tk)	0.359*** (5.24)	0.197*** (2.95)
Log MSME labor cost (Tk per year)	0.194** (2.48)	–
Log MSME other operating cost (Tk per year)	0.223*** (9.48)	–
Intercept	3.662** (2.42)	8.767*** (11.31)
R^2	0.411	0.967
N	888	888

MFS = mobile financial services; MSME = micro, small, and medium-sized enterprise.

Notes: Explanatory variables also include village-level variables. * and ** refer to statistical significance of 10% and 5%, respectively. Figures in parentheses are t-statistics based on robust standard errors clustered at the village level.

Source: Authors' calculations based on the ADB–BIDS Digital Microcredit Survey 2021.

Discussion

We examined the impact of MSME access to financial services (both institutional and mobile) on MSME productivity and income. There are two ways we can estimate ROA—through financial accounting data and estimating production and profit functions. According to financial data analysis, the ROA is as high as 53% for the MSME sector as a whole. In contrast, the rate of return to capital or asset is 38% when production function is used, and 22% when a profit function is estimated. As a profit function provides a more robust estimates of return to assets, we may use this as an indicator to determine if MSME is worth supporting by banks and MFIs (e.g., to finance startup or working-capital needs). Unfortunately, data show that own sources of finance is still the dominant form (87%) of startup capital with commercial banks not providing any financing in the MSME sector.

Since the MSME sector is still largely informal and involves small transactions, banks do not find them worthwhile to invest in. On the other hand, although MFIs extend short-term loans (repayable within a year), it can only help MSME's working capital needs. Moreover, many MFIs charge more than 22% interest on such short-term loans. Thus, it is obvious that MSMEs cannot rely on such a source for funding activities on a regular basis. As data show, 12% of MSMEs have an exclusive account with an MFI. But when MFS is included as an additional source of financial services (even if carrying out transactions such as repaying loans), many MSMEs have an MFS account. Data show that 47% of MSMEs have an account with both an MFI and MFS. Our estimates show that having an account with MFI yields an annual return of 4% above and beyond what is accounted for capital and other factors.

Thus, as financial accounting data show, the ROA is higher for MSMEs (54%) that have an MFI account against 36% for those who do not. However, microfinance is still nondigital and thus involves a high transaction cost for both lending and borrowing (e.g., costs of group-based weekly meetings and person-to person transaction cost of lending, repaying and depositing). But, our analysis shows, as only a small percentage of MSME are using MFS to pay off loans and deposit savings, we do not find any substantial benefit out of MFI account holders to interact with MFS. However, while MFS has been the fastest way of transferring money via cashless transfer mechanisms, it remains to be seen if MFI operations, including lending, are digitalized and if so, what it would mean to MSMEs in terms of productivity gains and income growth.

7. Assessing the Impact of Microenterprise on Rural Income: Does Access to Microfinance Matter?

The Role of Microenterprise in the Rural Economy

We have examined the role of finance (especially microfinance) in raising incomes and productivity in the microenterprise sector. However, the MSME sector is largely household-based and those households who carry out MSME activities are also sometimes engaged in non-MSME activities such as farming. So, the role of microfinance is underestimated if we do not examine its role in overall income and productivity for both groups of households—MSME and non-MSME households. MFIs lend as much as 50% of their loan portfolio to agriculture (see section 4), so it is important to assess the role of microfinance above and beyond microenterprises and the MSME sector.

Indeed, the literature rightly suggests that MSMEs account for a large share of rural nonfarm income and, hence, poverty reduction in Bangladesh (e.g., World Bank 2019, Khandker et al. 2016). As microfinance is still the major source of financial services for MSMEs, it is imperative that we determine how much microfinance accounts for variation in household income for both MSME and non-MSME households.

Before we estimate the impact of microfinance on overall household income as well as for MSME and non-MSME households separately, let us consider the distribution of rural income by sources, sector, and by two types of households (MSME and non-MSME). **Table 50** confirms that MSMEs account for a large share of rural income in the sample districts. We examined the distribution of income from different sources for three categories of households: (i) MSME households (those who are engaged in MSME activities), (ii) non-MSME households (those who are not engaged in any type of MSME activities), and (iii) households who are engaged in both MSME and non-MSME activities. Table 50 shows that MSME households are much better off than non-MSME households. The per capita income of an average MSME household is Tk8,652 versus Tk2,916 for non-MSME households, which means the average non-MSME household earns only one-third of the income of an average MSME household. The largest share of income for MSME households is from nonfarm sources (90%), while sources account for only 52% of income for an average non-MSME household. Interestingly, the MSME sector accounts for the largest share of total household income (85%) and the largest share of nonfarm income (94%). In terms of overall rural income, MSMEs account for 66% of nonfarm income, while nonfarm income accounts for 74% of household total income. Against this distribution of income by share of nonfarm in relation to farm sources, MSMEs account for 49% of overall rural income. No wonder the MSME sector is the main driver of income growth in the sample districts, a finding consistent with nationally representative data (Khandker et al. 2016, World Bank 2019).

Table 50: Distribution of Household Income by MSME Adoption Status

Welfare indicators	Households Engaged in MSME	Households not Engaged in MSME	Households Engaged in Both MSME and Other Sectors	All Households
Per capita income (Tk/month)	8,652.0	2,916.3	8,828.2	4,725.0
Per capita nonfarm income	7,806.8	1,519.2	7,780.6	3,501.9
Share of nonfarm income (Tk/month)	90.2	52.1	88.1	74.1
Share of MSME income in total income (%)	84.8	0	81.9	49.0
Share of MSME income in nonfarm income (%)	94.0	0	92.9	66.1
N	934	2,009	768	2,993

MSME = micro, small, and medium-sized enterprise.

Note: Nonfarm income includes non-earned income such as receipts from rent, transfer income, investment, pension, and remittance.

Source: Authors' calculations based on the ADB–BIDS Digital Microcredit Survey 2021.

Impact of Access to Financial Services on Household-Level Income and Productivity

Better access to finance, such as MFS in conjunction with an MFI, may affect income earned from both farm and nonfarm sources by both categories of households—households that adopted MSME as a source of income along with other non-MSME sources and households that do not rely on MSME but on other activities as a source of income. As MSMEs are largely household-based enterprises, it follows that better access to MFIs, the major financing agencies of different income-generating activities, cannot be evaluated only by limiting this impact evaluation to MSMEs. This is because many microenterprises are also engaged in farming and other categories of income-generating activities. Therefore, we need to evaluate the role of microfinance for income earning from alternative sources of income by MSME and non-MSME households, not only within the production function of MSME activities. Moreover, funds are fungible (i.e., financial services accessed through an MFI by an enterprise household can also be used for financing other income generating activities). So, it makes sense to evaluate microfinance in terms of its contribution to household welfare above and beyond its impact on enterprise-level income and productivity.

Consider the following reduced-form income equation (in semi-logarithmic form) with constrained-access to MFI functions:

$$lnY_{ij} = \beta_{0i} + \beta_1 X_{ij} + \beta_2 V_{ij} + \rho_i MF_{ij} + \varepsilon_{ij}, \qquad i \text{ denotes all households,} \qquad (6)$$

$$lnY_{kj} = \beta_{0k} + \beta_{1k} X_{kj} + \beta_{2k} V_{kj} + \rho_k MF_{kj} + \varepsilon_{kj}, \qquad k \text{ denotes MSME households only,} \qquad (7)$$

$$lnY_{lj} = \beta_{0l} + \beta_{1l} X_{lj} + \beta_{2l} V_{lj} + \rho_l MF_{lj} + \varepsilon_{il}, \qquad l \text{ denotes non-MSME households,} \qquad (8)$$

where Y's measure household income,[13] X's are household head's and other household characteristics, V measures vector of village-level attributes, MF measures access to microfinance (1= participates, 0 otherwise),[14] i denotes

---

[13] Total income can be broken into two major categories: farm and non-farm income. Income earned from an MSME belongs to nonfarm income. So, Y measures all three types of income (farm, nonfarm, and total).

[14] Alternatively, participation can be measured by the amount of borrowing from MFIs or transactions carried out with MFS. In this case, participation measures an average effect, while borrowing (transaction) measures marginal effect.

all categories of households, *k* denotes households who participate in MSME, and *l* measures those who do not participate in MSME sector for employment and income generation. β's are unknown coefficients to be estimated. Here ρ measures percentage change in household income if a household participates in MFI.

Equation (6) assumes that households can be combined to run income equation against MFI participation and other variables. In contrast, equations (7) and (8) assume that we cannot combine households by either having an MSME or not. That is, they need to be treated separately and we have to run a separate regression for the two groups of households. Running them separately, however, depends on the coefficient of the dummy (measuring if the household is engaged in microenterprise activity) if it is statistically significant in equation (6). We already found in section 6 that MSMEs and non-MSME households are not equivalent (i.e., they are not homogenous). This means we need to run equations (7) and (8) separately.

However, we run three models separately for all three categories of income. The results of equation (6) are presented in **Table 51**. As participation in MFIs, or both MFS and MFIs, is endogenously determined, we used predicted values instead of actual values in the regression.

Table 51: Impacts of Microfinance and Mobile Financial Services on Household Income—Two-Stage Estimation

Explanatory Variables	Log total income (Tk/month)	Log farm income (Tk/month)	Log nonfarm income (Tk/month)
Household participates in microfinance	0.028**	−0.042	0.062***
	(2.08)	(−1.27)	(2.89)
Household participates in microfinance X Household has MFS account	−0.001	−0.005	0.003
	(−0.70)	(−1.31)	(1.37)
Gender of HH head (Male=1, Female=0)	1.691**	1.647**	0.433
	(3.50)	(3.29)	(1.00)
Age of HH head (years)	−0.012	−0.04**	0.013*
	(−1.55)	(−3.46)	(1.81)
HH head completed primary level of education	−0.08	0.115	−0.513**
	(−0.51)	(0.40)	(−3.00)
HH head completed secondary level of education	−0.365	0.605	−1.026***
	(−1.27)	(1.13)	(−3.40)
HH head completed post-secondary level of education	−0.219	1.272**	−1.328***
	(−0.82)	(2.28)	(−3.88)
Number of adult males in HH	0.285**	1.006**	0.116
	(2.66)	(4.80)	(1.09)
Number of adult females in HH	0.124	0.366**	−0.034
	(1.44)	(2.03)	(−0.29)
Log HH agricultural land (decimals)	0.056*	−0.438**	0.436***
	(1.89)	(−6.85)	(9.00)
Log HH nonland asset (Tk)	0.331**	0.036	0.687***
	(4.49)	(0.34)	(7.38)
HH has grid electricity	0.273	0.693	0.308
	(1.00)	(1.55)	(0.81)
R^2	0.133	0.099	0.269
N	2,933	2,933	2,933

HH= household, MFS = mobile financial services.

Notes: Explanatory variables also include village-level variables. * and ** refer to statistical significance of 10% and 5%, respectively. Figures in parentheses are t-statistics based on robust standard errors clustered at the village level.

Source: Authors' calculations based on the ADB–BIDS Digital Microcredit Survey 2021.

The results indicate that the model accounts for 13% of variation in farm income, 10% in nonfarm income, and 27% in total income. In terms of overall fitness, a total income regression is preferred. Although MFS participation does not facilitate microfinance participation to have an additional effect on any type of income, MFI participation has a positive impact on total income as well as nonfarm income, without any significant effect on farm income. Specifically, household nonfarm income is about 6.2% higher for those households that participated in microfinance than those who did not participate. As a result, the total income of participating households is 3% higher on an average than that of nonparticipating households.

Table 52: Impacts of Microfinance and Mobile Financial Services on Income of MSME Households—Two-Stage Estimation

Explanatory Variables	Log total income (Tk/month)	Log farm income (Tk/month)	Log nonfarm income (Tk/month)
Household participates in microfinance	0.049	-0.139**	0.122**
	(1.20)	(-2.09)	(2.21)
Household participates in microfinance X Household has MFS account	-0.008	0.017	-0.009
	(-0.79)	(1.03)	(-0.80)
Gender of HH head (Male=1, Female=0)	0.783	-0.273	0.931
	(0.73)	(-0.40)	(0.77)
Age of HH head (years)	0.031**	0.005	0.028
	(2.12)	(0.37)	(1.57)
HH head completed primary level of education	-0.019	-0.173	0.023
	(-0.07)	(-0.60)	(0.06)
HH head completed secondary level of education	-0.577	-0.991*	-0.133
	(-1.40)	(-1.79)	(-0.24)
HH head completed post-secondary level of education	0.249	-0.530	0.762*
	(0.84)	(-1.14)	(1.82)
Number of adult males in HH	0.032	0.270	-0.028
	(0.15)	(1.11)	(-0.11)
Number of adult females in HH	-0.047	0.006	-0.024
	(-0.35)	(0.03)	(-0.13)
Log HH agricultural land (decimals)	-0.026	0.533**	-0.113
	(-0.54)	(7.10)	(-1.54)
Log HH nonland asset (Tk)	0.603***	0.895**	0.442**
	(4.47)	(6.12)	(2.80)
HH has grid electricity	0.693*	0.443	0.495
	(1.65)	(0.65)	(0.83)
R^2	0.127	0.307	0.050
N	934	934	934

HH = household; MFS = mobile financial services; MSME = micro, small, and medium-sized enterprise.

Notes: Explanatory variables also include village-level variables. * and ** refer to statistical significance of 10% and 5%, respectively. Figures in parentheses are t-statistics based on robust standard errors clustered at the village level.

Source: Authors' calculations based on the ADB–BIDS Digital Microcredit Survey 2021.

Table 52 and **Table 53** presents the regression results of model (7) and (8), respectively. This assumes that MSME participation is endogenous, just like the endogeneity of MFI participation. Using the predicted values of MFI participation and whether a household is engaged in MSME or not (using the results of section 5), we run equations (7) and (8). Results show that coefficients of MFI vary by the type of household. For example, MFI has a significant effect on only total income for non-MSME households. Thus, it increases total income of non-MSME households by about 4%. MFI participation has also differential impacts on farm and nonfarm income for two groups of households. For instance, while it reduces farm income for MSME households, it increases farm income for non-MSME households.[15] In contrast, MFI participation increases non-farm income by 12% for MSME households without affecting nonfarm income of non-MSME households. Therefore, increases in total household income due to MFI participation is derived from nonfarm sector for MSME households, while it is the opposite (i.e., mostly derived from farm sources) for non-MSME households. It supports the findings of descriptive analysis of the data presented in Table 50; that is, MSME households derive about 90% of their income from nonfarm sources, while non-MSME households derive only about 52% from nonfarm sources. Also, the net contribution of MFIs to overall rural income is about 9% (5% to MSME households and 4% to non-MSME households). This is higher than MFIs' net contribution of 4% to MSME revenue.

Table 53: Impacts of Microfinance and Mobile Financial Services on Income of Non-MSME Households—Two-Stage Estimation

Explanatory Variables	Log total income (Tk/month)	Log farm income (Tk/month)	Log nonfarm income (Tk/month)
Household participates in microfinance	0.035**	0.065**	−0.032
	(2.28)	(2.75)	(−0.96)
Household participates in microfinance X Household has MFS account	0.002*	−0.001	0.010**
	(1.69)	(−0.67)	(2.86)
Gender of HH head (Male=1, Female=0)	1.518**	0.847*	0.515
	(3.05)	(1.70)	(0.99)
Age of HH head (years)	−0.024**	0.011	−0.051**
	(−3.28)	(1.51)	(−4.63)
HH head completed primary level of education	−0.167	−0.644**	−0.084
	(−0.97)	(−3.00)	(−0.29)
HH head completed secondary level of education	−0.270	−0.938**	0.565
	(−0.84)	(−3.01)	(0.97)
HH head completed post-secondary level of education	−0.297	−1.816	1.802**
	(−0.84)	(−1.06)	(2.40)
Number of adult males in HH	0.388**	0.073	1.400**
	(3.82)	(0.53)	(6.33)
Number of adult females in HH	0.071	0.027	0.188
	(0.69)	(0.18)	(0.93)
Log HH agricultural land (decimals)	0.114**	0.363**	−0.459**
	(3.25)	(6.98)	(−5.88)
Log HH nonland asset (Tk)	0.160**	0.694**	−0.409**
	(1.99)	(6.16)	(−3.44)
HH has grid electricity	0.429	0.414	0.726*
	(1.46)	(1.04)	(1.66)
R^2	0.189	0.281	0.169
N	2,059	2,059	2,059

HH = household; MFS = mobile financial services; MSME = micro, small, and medium-sized enterprise.

Note: Explanatory variables also include village-level variables. * and ** refer to statistical significance of 10% and 5%, respectively. Figures in parentheses are t-statistics based on robust standard errors clustered at the village level.

Source: Authors' calculations based on the ADB–BIDS Digital Microcredit Survey 2021.

---

[15] It is a bit surprising to see that MFIs reduce the farm income of MSME households who derive more than 90% of their income from nonfarm sources. Thus, we may not be able to resolve the endogeneity of MFI participation completely.

One interesting result worth noting here is the facilitating role of mobile finance in income generation of MSME versus non-MSME households that both have access to microfinance. While MFS does not add value to any type of income of MSME households, it adds value to the income of non-MSME households who have an account with both MFS and MFI. That is, for microfinance participants, MFS increases total household income of non-MSME households by 0.2% of their total income via an increase in nonfarm income by 1%. Interestingly, even if MFI participation does not increase nonfarm income, it helps them to increase income from nonfarm sources via mobile financial services. It perhaps shows digitalization of microfinance matters even for non-MSME households by enhancing their participation in nonfarm activities.

Discussion

As MSME activities are largely household-based and many households engaged in MSME activities are also engaged in farm activities, it is important that improved access to financial services, such as having an account with MFIs, is evaluated not only against the productivity gains of MSMEs but also against overall income drawn from alternative sources. Data analysis shows that MSME households are better off than non-MSME households, enjoying at least three times the income of an average non-MSME household. Overall, MSMEs account for 66% of nonfarm income, while nonfarm income accounts for 74% of household income. MSMEs alone contribute about 49% of rural income. Our econometric analysis accounts for endogeneity due to self-selection into the MSME sector as well as having an account with an MFI. Results show that MFI account holders among MSME households gain up to 12% more income from nonfarm sources. Overall, rural households can gain up to a 5% increase in income from nonfarm sources and 4% from farm sources, resulting in an overall increase in per capita household income of 9%. Results also suggest a modest income gain from joint participation in an MFI and MFS, at least for the non-MSME households that are likely to gain by participating in nonfarm activities (not necessarily MSMEs).

8. Mitigating Risk in Microenterprise Production and Rural Income

Managing risk in production and income is always an intriguing issue for smallholders in agriculture and non-agriculture sectors alike. Management of risk in income or production also depends on how risk that affects production or income originates. Agriculture is always subject to high covariate risks due to weather and rainfall. However, risks originating in agriculture can also affect non-agriculture sectors, such as MSME activities, both directly and indirectly. It affects MSMEs directly because MSMEs engage in activities linked to agriculture for raw materials, and also because demand for their products is primarily from households engaged in agriculture. Agriculture affects MSMEs indirectly through covariate risks in production that MSMEs can be subjected to. Therefore, managing risk in MSMEs could be a double-edged sword for an entrepreneur.

However, managing risk in MSMEs also depends on the type of activities involved as some of them may be linked with urban market demand through backward linkages. In such an event, risk management can be diversified as it is a lot of easier for these enterprises compared with others that are largely dependent on agriculture and farming households. Risk management has been an important issue for all categories of microenterprises irrespective of backward or forward linkages over the COVID-19 pandemic period, which affected every sector and every source of income. Also, the pandemic has affected urban-based activities more than rural activities because of long period of lockdowns. Hence, it is important to learn in what ways MSMEs have been affected by COVID-19 and whether and how they have managed the risk caused by this pandemic.

Extent and Categories of Production Risk Faced by Microenterprises

Before we examine how COVID-19 has caused havoc in rural enterprises and rural households overall, let us consider the extent and categories of production risks for microenterprise and non-microenterprise households encountered in 2020/21. Table 54 shows it for both MSME and non-MSME households.

Table 54: Non-COVID-19 Shocks Faced by Households
(%)

Non-COVID-19 Shocks	MSME Households				Non-MSME Households	All Households
	Manufacturing	Business	Services	All Sectors		
Natural disasters	3.2	3.5	6.3	4.7	5.2	5.1
Losses in business	20.9	23.0	7.0	16.1	3.6	7.2
Employment loss among family members	0	10.5	15.7	12.2	11.3	11.5
Major illness or death among family members	20.3	17.8	21.3	19.4	21.9	21.2
Other losses	2.5	0.5	1.7	1.2	0.8	0.9
Any of the losses	36.2	40.5	39.8	40.0	34.5	36.1
N	45	452	391	888	2,197	3,085

COVID-19 = coronavirus disease; MSME = micro, small, and medium-sized enterprise.

Source: Authors' calculations based on the ADB–BIDS Digital Microcredit Survey 2021.

There are a range of shocks we considered—disasters triggered by natural hazards such as a cyclone and flooding, income and employment losses in businesses to which both natural and nonnatural factors contributed, health factors such as a major illness or death of family members, and other losses. About 36% of rural households—40% among MSMEs and 35% among non-MSME households—suffered shocks of any type over the 12 months preceding the survey. Among MSME households, the business sector was affected the most (40.5% versus an overall rate of 40.0% among MSME households). Data suggest that MSME households were affected more than non-MSME households, and that the business sector was affected the most among the three categories of MSMEs.

Among the risk factors, health risk affected the most respondents (21% overall, with 19% for MSME and 22% for non-MSME households) followed by employment loss (11.5% overall), income loss in business (7% overall), and disaster (5% overall). Among MSME households only, the most damaging source of risk after health factors were income loss in business (16%) and employment loss (12%).

Extent of COVID-19 Impact on Microenterprises' Losses

Households (both MSME and non-MSME) were asked more specifically how COVID-19 affected their income generation and other activities during the pandemic. **Table 55** presents the distribution of MSME and non-MSME households. Some 62% of the rural households (73% among MSME and 58% among non-MSME households) reported income losses during the pandemic compared with 42% overall (52% among MSME and 38% among non-MSME households) that reported employment losses due to COVID-19. Expenditure increases in regular consumption items (55% overall) and more specifically health expenses (20% overall) were the other major items that were affected by COVID-19.

Table 55: COVID-19-Related Impacts on Households
(%)

Non-COVID-19 Impact	MSME Households				Non-MSME Households	All Households
	Manufacturing	Business	Services	All Sectors		
HH members infected by COVID-19	0	1.7	0	0.9	0.5	0.6
High expense in medication and health supply	16.5	22.6	21.7	21.9	18.5	19.5

continued on next page

Table 55 continued

Non-COVID-19 Impact	MSME Households				Non-MSME Households	All Households
	Manufacturing	Business	Services	All Sectors		
High expense in health care	13.9	19.6	17.7	18.5	14	15.4
High expense for transport	11.4	3.5	1.9	3.2	4.4	4.0
High expense in consumption	54.5	48.1	54.1	51.0	56.6	55.0
High expense in raw materials	3.7	6.1	4.6	5.3	6.4	6.1
Income loss	87.4	73.2	70.5	72.7	57.7	62.1
Employment loss among family members	69.7	49.4	51.9	51.5	37.5	41.6
N	45	452	391	888	2,197	3,085

COVID-19 = coronavirus disease; HH = household; MSME = micro, small, and medium-sized enterprise.

Source: Authors' calculations based on the ADB–BIDS Digital Microcredit Survey 2021.

The pandemic equally affected both MSME and non-MSME households. That said, the major losers among rural households irrespective of sources of shocks (whether from COVID-19 or not) were the MSME households compared with non-MSME households. Since MSME households earn much more on average than non-MSME households (see section 7) and their income is more varying with respect to shocks, it follows that MSME households would be affected more than their counterpart non-MSME households due to health and non-health shocks caused by COVID-19. Also, we find that shocks, irrespective of whether it is health-related such as COVID-19 and non-health factors such as disaster, affect every category of MSME household equally.[16]

Coping with Risks Adversely Affecting Rural Enterprises and Households

What coping strategies did microenterprise and non-microenterprise households adopt to cope with such income and employment losses due to COVID-19? **Table 56** shows the distribution of households by all possible coping strategies they adopted last year. Rural households (irrespective of the source of income) rely more on their savings and assets (for sale) to cope with income and employment losses due to any shock. Specifically, 55% of rural households (70% among MSME households and 48% among non-MSME households) relied on own savings and assets to cope with any shock. Relatives and friends are the second category of support of coping for both categories of households. The third category of coping mechanism is cutting consumption—about 20% among all households (24% among MSME and 18% among non-MSME households) cut their food expenses as a measure of coping. Only 4% of households did not have to resort to any mechanism to cope with losses due to COVID-19 or non-COVID-19 shocks.

Government support during COVID-19 was of a little help—some 5% of all categories of households (6% among MSME and 4% among non-MSME households) received some government support in response to the pandemic. Nongovernment organization (NGO) support was also nominal (less than 1% reported as a source of coping). Some 6% of the households (6% each for MSME and non-MSME households) resorted to informal borrowing as a coping mechanism to weather both health and non-health shocks that caused income and employment losses due to the pandemic.

---

[16] It seems manufacturing was slightly more affected by COVID-19 than other activities.

Table 56: Coping Mechanisms Adopted by Households
(%)

Measure to Cope with COVID-19	MSME Households				Non-MSME Households	All Households
	Manufacturing	Business	Services	All Sectors		
Savings	70.3	61.1	51.4	57.4	40.4	45.4
Sell asset	17.1	11.1	14.1	12.7	7.6	9.1
Relatives and friends	15.5	15.9	23.9	19.3	19.8	19.7
Govt. assistance	0	5.6	6.3	5.6	4.3	4.7
NGO support	5.3	1.5	0.6	1.3	0.6	0.8
Informal borrowing	9.7	5.9	5.1	5.8	6.2	6.1
Cut food expense	26.5	20.8	27.6	24	17.6	19.5
Other mechanism	8.9	11.7	6.6	9.4	7.8	8.3
None	4.3	1.9	4.1	3.0	3.7	3.5
N	45	452	391	888	2,197	3,085

COVID-19 = coronavirus disease; MSME = micro, small, and medium-sized enterprise; NGO = nongovernment organization.

Source: Authors' calculations based on the ADB–BIDS Digital Microcredit Survey 2021.

Estimates of the Impact of COVID-19 on Microenterprise Income and Productivity

As mentioned, MSME households on average were hurt more from COVID-19, and so it is important to estimate the extent of the losses in terms of its impact on income and productivity of MSME. That is, we estimate the net effect of COVID or any other exogenous health shocks on an enterprise's revenue and profit. This necessitates estimating the Cobb–Douglas type revenue function of equation (4) and profit function of equation (5), where the extent of village level COVID-19 incidence or any household-level health shocks measured by the incidence of illness or death of any family member can be treated as additional regressor. Since they are treated as exogenous to enterprise-level decision-making, they enter the equation as exogenous without any issue of endogeneity. Consider the following augmented production function in equation (9) and profit function in equation (10) with two additional regressors:

$$lnQ_{ij} = \alpha_0 lnA + \alpha lnK_{ij} + \beta lnL_{ij} + \gamma lnR_{ij} + \mu^q H_{ij} + \theta^q C_j + \varepsilon_{ij} \qquad (9)$$

$$lnP_{ij} = \equiv \alpha_0 lnA + \alpha lnK_{ij} + \mu^p H_{ij} + \theta^p C_j + \pi_{ij} \qquad (10)$$

where H_{ij} measures health shocks of household members, C_j indicates the incidence of COVID-19 in the village, and μ and θ are unknown coefficients to be estimated. The other variables and coefficients are defined as before.

Table 57 presents the production and profit estimates of the COVID-19 and non-COVID-19 health shocks on microenterprise income and productivity. We find that there is about a 20% reduction in profit due to non-COVID-19 health factors. In contrast, COVID-19 caused a 22% reduction in profit and a 15% reduction in revenue for an average microenterprise. This represents an adverse net impact of COVID-19 on microenterprise productivity, confirming a priori expectations that COVID-19 caused losses in the MSME sector.

Table 57: Impacts of COVID-19 and Non-COVID-19 Health Shocks on MSME Income and Productivity

Explanatory Variables	Log revenue (Tk/year)	Log profit (Tk/year)
Household suffered from non-COVID-19 related major illness and death in last 12 months	-0.056	-0.205*
	(-0.69)	(-1.75)
Village was affected by COVID-19 pandemic	-0.152*	-0.218**
	(-1.91)	(-2.47)
Gender of MSME operator (Male=1, Female=0)	0.115	0.106
	(0.67)	(0.58)
Age of MSME operator (years)	-0.001	-0.007*
	(-0.47)	(-1.76)
MSME operator completed primary level of education	-0.047	-0.060
	(-0.58)	(-0.66)
MSME operator completed secondary level of education	0.126	-0.547**
	(0.81)	(-2.05)
MSME operator completed post-secondary level of education	0.290***	-0.105
	(2.30)	(-0.66)
MSME activity is business	-0.137	0.273
	(-0.49)	(1.10)
MSME operator is services	-0.005	0.263
	(-0.02)	(0.93)
MSME is household-based	0.190	0.490***
	(1.58)	(2.61)
MSME is operated in commercial location	0.281**	0.391**
	(2.14)	(2.08)
Log MSME capital (Tk)	0.375***	0.219***
	(5.42)	(3.14)
Log MSME labor cost (Tk/year)	0.190**	
	(2.41)	–
Log MSME other operating cost (Tk/year)	0.226***	
	(9.63)	–
Intercept	3.451**	8.604***
	(2.31)	(10.75)
R^2	0.409	0.967
N	888	888

COVID-19 = coronavirus disease; MSME = micro, small, and medium-sized enterprise.

Note: Explanatory variables also include village-level variables. * and ** refer to statistical significance of 10% and 5%, respectively. Figures in parentheses are t-statistics based on robust standard errors clustered at the village level.

Source: Authors' calculations based on the ADB–BIDS Digital Microcredit Survey 2021.

Risk Mitigation

Given the extent of COVID-19 prevalence and its adverse impacts on MSME productivity, it is important to determine what risk mitigating strategies if any adopted by the enterprises to weather the pandemic. This requires an estimation of models (9) and (10) with at least two mitigating avenues: government support and MFI participation. We include these two factors directly in the above equations and then their interactions with government support dummy (whether a household received any government or NGO support to cope with COVID-19) and MFI participation dummy (whether the MSME has an account with an MFI).[17]

---

[17]   Although government support is exogenous, MFI participation is endogenous. So, a predicted value of MFI participation is used instead.

Table 58 presents the results. We find that while MFI participation has positive effect on MSME revenue, government or NGO support—either independently or when interacted with shock—does not have any statistically significant effect on MSME income and productivity. This implies that institutional assistance during the pandemic was perhaps not adequate.

Table 58: Role of Microcredit and Institutional Supports in Mitigating Shocks and COVID-19 Impacts on MSME Productivity

Explanatory Variables	Log Revenue (Tk/year)	Log Profit (Tk/year)
Household suffered from non-COVID-19 related major illness and death in last 12 months	0.024 (0.22)	−0.211 (−1.34)
Village was affected by COVID-19 pandemic	−0.082 (−0.81)	−0.103 (−0.82)
Household participates in microfinance	0.037** (2.00)	0.029 (1.39)
Household suffered from non-COVID-19 related major illness and death in last 12 months x Household participates in microfinance	−0.030 (−0.60)	−0.001 (−0.01)
Village was affected by COVID-19 pandemic x Household participates in microfinance	−0.026 (−0.95)	−0.048 (−1.22)
Household received government or NGO support during COVID-19 pandemic	0.321 (1.44)	0.185 (1.25)
Household suffered from non-COVID-19 related major illness and death in last 12 months x Household received government or NGO support during the COVID-19 pandemic	−0.157 (−0.77)	0.094 (0.45)
Village was affected by COVID-19 pandemic X Household received government or NGO support during COVID-19 pandemic	−0.117 (−0.41)	0.214 (0.91)
Gender of MSME operator (Male=1, Female=0)	0.110 (0.64)	0.101 (0.54)
Age of MSME operator (years)	−0.002 (−0.63)	−0.007* (−1.83)
MSME operator completed primary level of education	−0.042 (−0.53)	−0.050 (−0.56)
MSME operator completed secondary level of education	0.102 (0.66)	−0.551** (−2.08)
MSME operator completed post-secondary level of education	0.291*** (2.41)	−0.099 (−0.64)
MSME activity is business	−0.122 (−0.46)	0.313 (1.29)
MSME operator is services	0.006 (0.02)	0.289 (1.03)
MSME is household-based	0.168 (1.39)	0.475*** (2.55)
MSME is operated in commercial location	0.269** (2.07)	0.388** (2.10)
Log MSME capital (Tk)	0.376*** (5.43)	0.218*** (3.08)
Log MSME labor cost (Tk/year)	0.191** (2.39)	–

continued on next page

Table 58 continued

Explanatory Variables	Log Revenue (Tk/year)	Log Profit (Tk/year)
Log MSME other operating cost (Tk/year)	0.226***	
	(10.01)	–
Intercept	3.418**	8.533***
	(2.28)	(10.24)
R²	0.417	0.968
N	888	888

COVID-19 = coronavirus disease; MSME = micro, small, and medium-sized enterprise; NGO = nongovernment organization.

Note: Explanatory variables also include village-level variables. * and ** refer to statistical significance of 10% and 5%, respectively. Figures in parentheses are t-statistics based on robust standard errors clustered at the village level.

Source: Authors' calculations based on the ADB–BIDS Digital Microcredit Survey 2021.

Discussion

We discussed the extent of adverse effects caused by the COVID-19 pandemic on MSME sector and see if government stimulus money had any meaningful benefits in mitigating the adverse effects of COVID-19 or other health shocks on MSME activities as well as the NGO support in weathering the negative effects of COVID-19, if any, on income and productivity. Data analysis shows that a large percentage of households (both MSME or non-MSME) lost income and employment due to the COVID-19 pandemic, but only a very few received government or NGO support to cope with the adverse effects. This is more so for MSME households relying on nonfarm sources of income and less for non-MSME households who rely less on nonfarm sources.

We find that COVID-19 caused at least 20% loss to profit or income for microentrepreneurs on average. This is a substantial loss incurred by the MSME sector. The results also confirm that government stimulus did not reach them adequately. So, risk mitigation was not possible and, hence, many households had to reduce consumption or use savings to weather the pandemic.

9. Conclusion

This baseline study was carried out for the purpose of a full-scale randomized controlled trial (RCT) study on the digitalization of microfinance in Bangladesh. The data collection, carried out during the months of October–December 2021, comprised a variety of information to investigate several issues including a study of the possible role of microfinance and mobile financial services in microenterprise operations and their impact on microenterprise productivity. It was also designed to study the extent and nature of losses incurred by the microenterprise sector and rural households in general due to the COVID-19 pandemic. The baseline study therefore covers issues such as how microfinance borrowers among MSMEs were affected by the COVID-19 pandemic health-wise and economically; how microfinance transactions were affected (e.g., loans, repayments, and savings) by the MFS services available; how micro-entrepreneurs' income-generating activities, which are supported by MFIs, were affected; how MFI branch activities were affected; and whether or not some kind of digitalized services were offered during this pandemic, and so on.

In this study, we survey households and communities with and without access to microfinance and mobile financial services that help assess the impact of microfinance and MFS in its current form on MSME productivity and income. The survey collected information from 2,993 households from 124 villages and communities exposed to the pandemic in 2020/21. Thus, we can evaluate the consequences of the recent pandemic on the performance of the MSME sector, and in turn, its impact on household welfare. Like almost any country in the world, Bangladesh witnessed a serious economic slowdown due to the COVID-19 pandemic, and hence, the baseline survey was planned to assess the potential impact of the pandemic: (i) to what extent the pandemic has caused disruptions in overall well-being including the income and productivity of MFI entrepreneurs, and (ii) whether and how government and other assistance offered during this difficult time was successful in mitigating the negative consequences as experienced by the MSME sector and its beneficiaries.

There was a variety of information collected on households, MFIs, communities, and MSME owners that are the basis for drawing a randomly selected sample for carrying out the proposed RCT design of a digitalized version of microfinance that would be introduced later in 2022. And a midline and an endline survey will be carried out subsequently after the intervention is introduced to evaluate its impact and cost-effectiveness.

The baseline survey was carried out encompassing several stakeholders engaged in the MSME and MFI sectors. To draw the sample for this RCT piloting, we carried out a village census in the randomly selected villages of Rangpur division, where the incidence of both poverty and microfinance operations is high. A village census helps us draw a sample of 2,993 households from 124 villages where households randomly drawn consist of the following categories—those already participating in MFI activities, those willing to participate, and those not willing to participate. Villages were drawn randomly from the list of villages in five districts from Rangpur division. Also, household survey data show that MSME sector distribution (manufacturing, business, and services) follows a pattern observed at the national level. Therefore, the data collected from Rangpur division consists of a representative sample of (i) households with and without access to microfinance, and (ii) households with and without MSME engagement. The data also consist of branch-level operations of major MFIs active in the sampled villages that helped analyze whether COVID-19 has affected MFI performances.

Data analysis suggests that MSMEs are largely home-based and informal. Only a fraction of the MSME sector is in manufacturing, with business and services overwhelmingly representing the sector. MSME owners draw income from both farm and nonfarm sources; yet, MSMEs account for 90% of their income. Overall, nonfarm sources contribute 49% to rural income and MSMEs account as much as 69% of rural nonfarm income. Microenterprises have access to both MFIs and MFS but not much access to commercial banks. About 71% of microenterprises have an account with MFIs, while only 19% of MSMEs have an account with a commercial bank. MSMEs can also have an MFS account to help them carry out cashless transactions such as money transfers or payments.

The startup capital of MSMEs comes mainly from own sources; institutional sources such as banks and MFIs hardly provide startup capital to the sector. Yet, we find that the ROA in microenterprise activities is as low as 22% and as high as 37%, suggesting there is no reason for banks not to finance MSME activities. On the other hand, MFIs supporting MSMEs by extending short-term loans (often repayable within a year) only support the working capital needs of MSMEs. We find that returns are subject to credit constraints, suggesting that better access to finance can enhance enterprise-level productivity. Indeed, our research shows that better access to credit, measured by whether an MSME has an account with an MFI, enhances both firm-level productivity and household-level income.

It follows therefore that it is not the lack of income-earning opportunities in the MSME sector that constrains growth in this sector. In fact, it is lack of better access to both institutional and digital financial services that constrain the expansion and productivity of this sector.

The major outstanding issues involving MSME sector growth and productivity are therefore twofold: (i) when and how commercial banks could be attracted to support MSME sector growth, and (ii) how MFIs can be persuaded to utilize digital technology to support cashless transactions for both loan repayment and savings deposit, while also lending money digitally. As it stands, manufacturing, which is more registered and hence, is formal, attracts more loans from commercial banks than informal sector MSMEs involved in business or services. So, enhanced registration of MSME activities is perhaps a way to attract commercial banks to support MSME sectoral growth.

On the other hand, as MFIs involve high transaction costs due to a small amount of transactions per customer and per loan, one way to reduce the cost of borrowing is finding out how such high transaction costs can be reduced. MFS, which cover both rural and urban areas as well as the formal and informal sectors, are a very cost-effective way of carrying out transactions (e.g., transferring money) efficiently and reliably. As of now, mobile finance is hardly utilized for microlending in Bangladesh. So, for better access to and improved efficiency of microfinance lending to MSMEs, there is no substitute for digitalizing microfinance and, hence, digitalizing MSME financing in the process.

There is another way the digitalization of microfinance can help attract commercial banks' entry into this sector. If the digitalization of microfinance helps boost MSME productivity and growth, this would also help MSMEs become formal entities by enhancing the registration process. Commercial banks would be attracted to compete with MFIs in extending financial services to the MSME sector. So, competition can reduce the interest rates charged by MFIs, since commercial bank lending rates are much lower than those of MFIs.

Digitalization of financial services would also be a win–win situation for the sector for yet another reason. Commercial lending to the informal sector has already started via mobile financial technology. In December 2021, a local commercial bank, City Bank, launched digital loans for bKash users who have registered with bKash through the biometric system (e-KYC) on 15 December 2021. Only those who use the bKash app and carry out various types of transactions regularly are eligible for this loan. These bKash app users can take instant loans with just a few clicks in the loans section in the bKash app. No documents, nominee, or guarantor is required to take this loan. Through this new service, Bangladesh has entered the era of digital microfinance. Eligible bKash users get a loan of Tk500–Tk20,000 at a 9% interest rate. The maximum repayment duration of the loan is 3 months. An artificial intelligence system determines who will get the loan by reviewing their past bKash transactions. The bKash app can "re-register" through e-KYC those who have completed know-your-customer registration in the traditional way and subsequently become bKash users. It is then possible that the same type of technology can be utilized by Grameen Bank, BRAC, ASA, and other MFIs to offer financial services, including loans to their clients, using such a proven digital technology.

Better access to finance therefore means both offering financial services covering a variety of services, such as extending both short- and long-term loans at affordable prices, and providing digital financial services (mobile and online services) through digitalization of financial services such as microfinance, the largest lender supporting the MSME sector, as well as commercial banks extending services to the MSME sector. It is in this sense that a study is worth supporting to explore whether the digitalization of financial services extended to MSMEs is feasible, and if it is, what it would mean to providers and users alike and how it could affect MSME productivity and improve the welfare of the entire population. The baseline data collection is thus directed precisely to achieve these core research objectives.

Appendix
Sample Design and Data Collection and Description

Sampling Design

The study design consists of four survey instruments: (i) village census; (ii) household survey, which includes detailed sections on microenterprise activities; (iii) community survey; and (iv) survey of selected branches of microfinance institutions (MFIs). Based on the latest Household Income and Expenditure Survey (HIES) poverty map of the Bangladesh Bureau of Statistics, Rangpur division is the most backward region in the country and, hence, was selected for the microenterprise study (see the poverty map Figure A.1 drawn on latest district-wise poverty estimates by the Bangladesh Bureau of Statistics). More specifically, the sampling frame designed and adopted is the following:

1. Five districts in this division have been selected based on the latest HIES poverty map (over 40% head count ratio) and over 60% of micro, small, and medium-sized enterprise (MSME) coverage (2013 economic census): Dinajpur, Gaibandha, Kurigram, Lalmonirhat, and Rangpur (see **Figure A.2** in the Appendix for district-wise count of MFIs).

2. Also, selection of villages in these five districts was done following the HIES sampling strategy (for comparability) that draws a random list of 36 villages in each district. As this results in 180 villages in total, we have decided to drop 6 villages randomly from 36 villages from each district. So, we selected 150 villages randomly from this list of 180 villages. Based on the consideration of budget and time, we decided to carry out the survey only in 124 villages (see, the list of villages for each in **Table A.1** in the Appendix).

3. A census listing was carried out in 124 randomly selected villages from these five districts.

4. Using village census information, a list of eligible households who qualify to participate in the proposed microfinance treatment was prepared from which 25 households were randomly drawn from each village with proportional representation of eligible and non-eligible households.

5. Households are defined as eligible who are already MFI members of any of the three major MFIs active in the sampled villages plus those who are willing to participate in MFI but are not currently members of any MFI, while also holding less than 50 decimals of agricultural landholding. Households are defined as noneligible who are holding more than 50 decimals of agricultural landholding and not currently members of MFIs. The distribution of 25 randomly drawn households from each village was the following: 12 households were randomly selected from the current participants of three major programs (ASA, BRAC, and GB); 7 households from the list of the target and willing to participate; 3 households from nontarget but willing to participate; and 3 households from those nonwilling to participate in any microfinance program.

6. Because of the predominance of MSMEs among MFI-participating households and those households who are engaged in rural non-agricultural activities, this sampling design was expected to capture enough variations of

households in terms of MSME and MFI membership.[18] Sampling weights are used in estimation where weights are calculated based on the village distribution of eligible and noneligible households as well as MFI participating and non-participating households.

Thus, a total of 3,100 (25 households drawn from each of 124 villages) with the distribution of 1,488 households were selected from the list of current participation of the three major MFIs (ASA, BRAC, and GB); 831 households from the list of eligible and willing to participate; 372 households from nontarget willing to participate; and 372 households from the list of non-willing to participate. However, because of data inconsistency, 107 households were dropped eventually from the listed 3,100 households. Hence, a total of 2,993 households were ultimately selected for detailed data collection and analysis. The distribution of 2,993 households is shown in **Table A.2** in the Appendix.

Why Is Baseline Data Important?

The village census data helps carry out the following research objectives: (i) identify the extent of program eligibility and MSME engagement among households interviewed as part of the village census; (ii) examine the extent of coverage of microfinance in MSME operations and its induced impact in supporting MSMEs and enhancing income and productivity of the entrepreneurs; (iii) evaluate the performance of MFIs operating in the study villages in terms of their loan disbursement, deposit mobilization, loan outstanding, and interest income and administrative cost involved in their operational efficiency; (iv) identify the impact of pandemic, if any, on the performances of MFIs and MSME sector as a whole defined in terms of losses in income and productivity; and (v) determine whether mobile financial services (MFS) and government stimulus offered during the pandemic played any role in mitigating induced negative consequences.

Village Census Questionnaires

A village census questionnaire was administered in each village with the sole purpose of identifying the distribution of eligible (to be treated with some kind of microfinance program—digital or nondigital) and noneligible households. Eligibility is defined by two ways—either they are members of one of three major MFIs operating in the village, or households who are eligible to participate in any of these three MFIs (membership is exogenously defined by whether they are holding less than 50 decimals of land) and willing to participate. So, the census questionnaire asks each household head (besides their age, gender, education, and main occupation) about the extent of their agricultural landholding (this does not include homestead land). Besides microfinance eligibility, the census questionnaire asks each household head if any member is primarily engaged in any of three major MSME activities (manufacturing, business, and services). The census question also seeks to identify if the household owns any mobile phone and if any member has an MFS account. Therefore, the census questionnaire provides an opportunity for identifying the extent of MFI membership by program and MSME coverage and its sectoral distribution in household employment, as well as the extent of MFS coverage. Finally, village census is used to create the sample frame for sampling households.

Multitopic Household Survey Questionnaires

The household questionnaires served three purposes: (i) identify the pretreatment status of households and individuals in terms of income, consumption, employment, MFI membership; and other major indicators of welfare;

---

[18]   More than 60% of rural households draw more than 80% of their income from rural nonfarm activities.

(ii) provide data to evaluate the existing role of microfinance and digitalization (e.g., MFS) in the MSME sector as well as income and other indicators of household and individual welfare; and (iii) provide information about the extent of losses in income and consumption due to COVID-19 and the roles of alternative factors including the government stimulus in mitigating the crisis.

Given the scope of the study, a multi-topic household survey was designed with 14 major topics covering a range of issues central to the understanding of who does what, with what resources, and what this means to individual and household income, productivity, consumption, and other indicators of well-being. More importantly, as microenterprise activities, which are mostly carried out at households or in the marketplace, are also covered in this multi-topic household survey. Employment (either self- or wage-employment) in both farm and nonfarm activities are covered with detailed information on the production data on both farming and nonfarming activities. Income data was collected for farm and nonfarm sources including production and cost information involved in carrying out these production activities. Borrowing data collected for borrowing from different sources and purposes of the loans. The questionnaires also collected information about government stimulus and microfinance and mobile financial services, which help address what roles government and other institutions played in improving individual and household welfare. Data were also collected about households' and business' exposure to different shocks including coronavirus disease (COVID-19) and possible income and employment losses. Survey also collects information on household and business's coping strategies including remittance and public support if any to cope with the losses.

Community Questionnaire

Community characteristics and infrastructures (e.g., paved roads, schools, banks, and markets) can play a role in determining household welfare, above and beyond household characteristics, abilities and whatever interventions households receive. That is why it is important to control for community characteristics when we would like to estimate the impacts of microcredit interventions. With that purpose in mind, the study will also carry out a community survey in the studied villages.

Branch-Level Surveys of Microfinance Institutions

The major thrust of the study is to determine the nature and extent of microfinance role in income generating of rural enterprises, especially of the cottage and small enterprises. Besides asking the household about MFI involvement and its status in generating income and employment during the pandemic year, we also survey the designated branches of MFIs currently operating in our study villages. Why are we interested in branch operation of MFIs? The yearly annual reports of major MFIs active in our study villages (ASA, BRAC and GB) over the last 3 years can provide us MFI coverage (e.g., sectoral and gender-wise) and financial efficiency before and during the pandemic. However, they do not help us determine the factors (both economic and noneconomic including infrastructures) influencing their efficiency in terms of outreach as well as financial and economic efficiency. The branch-level operation of three major MFIs active in 124 surveyed villages will help us determine this.

So, the MFI questionnaires, besides identifying its location and distance from the surveyed villages, ask questions concerning six major features of MFI operation: (i) outreach in terms of membership and borrowers by males and females; (ii) characteristics of branches in terms of location and staff and managers running the branches; (iii) interest charged on loans by sector and types of loans (e.g., emergency loans and general loans) and interest rates on deposits; (iv) costs of operation such as staff cost, rental, utility, and loan default rates; (v) extent of digitalization of branch operation already done and what does it cover; (vi) distribution of loan disbursement and outstanding over the last 3 years by gender of loan recipients and major sectors; and (vii) savings deposits under alternative categories (voluntary versus involuntary member savings).

Discussion

The primary objectives of the baseline survey are fivefold: (i) create a baseline survey for designing and implementing a randomized controlled trial design to study the benefits of digitalization of microfinance; (ii) determine the role of microfinance in the current structure of household income (from both farm and nonfarm activities) and its induced impact on household consumption and other indicators of welfare; (iii) examine the scope of digitalization (defined primarily in terms of mobile financial services) already in place and determine whether it has encompassed into some type of microfinance operation (e.g., savings mobilization and loan repayments); (iv) identify the role of MSMEs in household income and employment; and (v) investigate the negative impact of COVID-19 and the role of government, if any, in mitigating negative consequences on business profits and household income and productivity.

The baseline data are used to understand microenterprise development and the role of microfinance in its development. This is to analyze issues (ii)–(v) outlined above to determine the scope of microfinance in microenterprise development and the scope of digitalization of microfinance in furthering the growth of MSME sector. However, the analysis depends on good quality data and its generation is very much context specific. That is, quality of data matters a lot, and hence, the research team took utmost effort to ensure good quality data collection and its administration by well-trained enumerators.

Table A.1: List of Villages Sampled for Household Survey

Zila	Upazila	Union	Village
Dinajpur	Biral	Biral	Biral
Dinajpur	Biral	Biral	Sankarpur
Dinajpur	Biral	Dharmapur	Pirojpur
Dinajpur	Biral	Sahargram	Atghera
Dinajpur	Birampur	Benail	Chautha
Dinajpur	Birampur	Katla	Shoilen
Dinajpur	Birganj	Maricha	Katgar
Dinajpur	Birganj	Nijpara	Kaikuri
Dinajpur	Birganj	Shatagram	Kashimnagar
Dinajpur	Birganj	Sujalpur	Jagdal part
Dinajpur	Bochaganj	Ishania	Khamar khanpur
Dinajpur	Chirirbandar	Isabpur	Naokhair
Dinajpur	Dinajpur sadar	Auliapur	Saidpur
Dinajpur	Dinajpur sadar	Kamalpur	Dakshin maheshpur
Dinajpur	Dinajpur sadar	Sekhpura	Madhabpur
Dinajpur	Fulbari	Daulatpur	Barui para
Dinajpur	Fulbari	Shibnagar	Debipur (purbapara)
Dinajpur	Hakimpur	Boaldar	Boigram
Dinajpur	Khansama	Bhabki	Chaknia
Dinajpur	Khansama	Khamar para	Duhasuha

continued on next page

Table A.1 continued

Zila	Upazila	Union	Village
Dinajpur	Nawabganj	Bhaduria	Dighiratna
Dinajpur	Nawabganj	Kushdaha	Rahimapur
Dinajpur	Parbatipur	Habra	Sherpur
Dinajpur	Parbatipur	Manmathapur	Khorakhai
Dinajpur	Parbatipur	Mostafapur	Mohapur (mahabpur)
Gaibandha	Fulchhari	Erendabari	Char harichandi
Gaibandha	Fulchhari	Kanchi para	Bhasar para
Gaibandha	Gaibandha sadar	Badiakhali	Pathandanga
Gaibandha	Gaibandha sadar	Ballamjhar	Dhanghara (part)
Gaibandha	Gaibandha sadar	Boali	Nasaratpur
Gaibandha	Gaibandha sadar	Kamarjani	Karaibari
Gaibandha	Gaibandha sadar	Lakshmipur	Khurda malibari
Gaibandha	Gaibandha sadar	Ramchandrapur	Ramchandrapur
Gaibandha	Gobindaganj	Darbasta	Sinjani
Gaibandha	Gobindaganj	Harirampur	Sonaidanga baikunthap
Gaibandha	Gobindaganj	Katabari	Bogdaha
Gaibandha	Gobindaganj	Mahimaganj	Panthamari
Gaibandha	Gobindaganj	Rakhal buruz	Rakhal buruz
Gaibandha	Gobindaganj	Shakhahar	Sihigaon
Gaibandha	Palashbari	Barisal	Paschim gopinathpur
Gaibandha	Palashbari	Hossainpur	Ramkrishnapur
Gaibandha	Palashbari	Manoharpur	Ghorabandha
Gaibandha	Sadullapur	Banagram	Jayenpur
Gaibandha	Sadullapur	Banagram	Manduar
Gaibandha	Sadullapur	Dhaperhat	Mangala para
Gaibandha	Sadullapur	Jamalpur	Daudpur
Gaibandha	Sadullapur	Naldanga	Naldanga
Gaibandha	Saghata	Bonar para	Raghabpur
Gaibandha	Saghata	Padumsahar	Chalk datia
Gaibandha	Sundarganj	Dahabanda	Jhinia
Gaibandha	Sundarganj	Shantiram	Paran
Kurigram	Bhurungamari	Pathardubi	Maidan
Kurigram	Chilmari	Ashtamir char	Natarkandi
Kurigram	Chilmari	Thanahat	Putimari
Kurigram	Kurigram sadar	Bhogdanga	Char baraibari
Kurigram	Kurigram sadar	Ghogadaha	Raulia
Kurigram	Kurigram sadar	Kanthalbari	Harishwar kalua
Kurigram	Kurigram sadar	Punchgachhi	Chhatrapur
Kurigram	Kurigram sadar	Ward no-03	Paschim sabuj para
Kurigram	Kurigram sadar	Ward no-09	Doctor para
Kurigram	Phulbari	Bhanagmore	Suzanerkuti
Kurigram	Phulbari	Naodanga	Khalisha kotal
Kurigram	Rajarhat	Chakirpashar	Joydeb hayat
Kurigram	Rajarhat	Gharialdanga	Khitab khan

continued on next page

Table A.1 continued

Zila	Upazila	Union	Village
Kurigram	Rajarhat	Rajarhat	Sadagar
Kurigram	Ulipur	Bazra	Sadua damarhat
Kurigram	Ulipur	Daldalia	Uttar daldalia
Kurigram	Ulipur	Durgapur	Durgapur
Kurigram	Ulipur	Gunaigachh	Rajballabh
Kurigram	Ulipur	Pandul	Tanuram
Kurigram	Ulipur	Thetroy	Dari kishorepur
Lalmonirhat	Aditmari	Bhelabari	Bhelabari
Lalmonirhat	Aditmari	Durgapur	Durgapur
Lalmonirhat	Aditmari	Kamalabari	Chandanpati
Lalmonirhat	Aditmari	Palashi	Baraibari
Lalmonirhat	Aditmari	Saptibari	Khata para
Lalmonirhat	Aditmari	Sarpukur	Saral khan
Lalmonirhat	Hatibandha	Barakhata	Purba saradubi
Lalmonirhat	Hatibandha	Daoabari	Purba bichhandai
Lalmonirhat	Hatibandha	Goddimari	Madhya goddimari
Lalmonirhat	Hatibandha	Nowdabash	Ketkibari
Lalmonirhat	Kaliganj	Chalbala	Chalbala madanpur
Lalmonirhat	Kaliganj	Chandrapur	Satirpar
Lalmonirhat	Kaliganj	Dalagram	Uttar dalagram
Lalmonirhat	Kaliganj	Kakina	Gopal roy
Lalmonirhat	Kaliganj	Madati	Khalisha madati
Lalmonirhat	Kaliganj	Tushbhandar	Dakshin ghanashyam
Lalmonirhat	Kaliganj	Tushbhandar	Kashiram
Lalmonirhat	Lalmonirhat sadar	Barabari	Khedabagh
Lalmonirhat	Lalmonirhat sadar	Gokunda	Ratipur
Lalmonirhat	Lalmonirhat sadar	Harati	Kismat harati
Lalmonirhat	Lalmonirhat sadar	Khuniagachh	Khuniagachh
Lalmonirhat	Lalmonirhat sadar	Mahendranagar	Teli para
Lalmonirhat	Lalmonirhat sadar	Mogalhat	Batrish hazari
Lalmonirhat	Lalmonirhat sadar	Mogalhat	Phulgachh
Lalmonirhat	Lalmonirhat sadar	Rajpur	Changra
Lalmonirhat	Patgram	Baura	Nabinagar
Rangpur	Badarganj	Damodarpur	Mostafapur
Rangpur	Badarganj	Lohani para	Kanchabari
Rangpur	Gangachara	Alam biditar	Alam biditar
Rangpur	Gangachara	Gangachara	Arazi niamat
Rangpur	Gangachara	Kolkanda	Dakshin kolkanda
Rangpur	Kaunia	Haragachh	Sonatan
Rangpur	Kaunia	Shahidbagh	Khurda bhutchhara
Rangpur	Mitha pukur	Bara hazratpur	Askarpur
Rangpur	Mitha pukur	Chengmari	Harar para
Rangpur	Mitha pukur	Durgapur	Chithali dakshinpara
Rangpur	Mitha pukur	Emadpur	Rahmatpur

continued on next page

Table A.1 continued

Zila	Upazila	Union	Village
Rangpur	Mitha pukur	Khoragachh	Siraj
Rangpur	Mitha pukur	Mayenpur	Jagadishpur
Rangpur	Pirganj	Chaitrakul	Ramchandrapur
Rangpur	Pirganj	Madankhali	Khayerbari
Rangpur	Pirganj	Roypur	Dhulgari
Rangpur	Pirganj	Tukuria	Taraf mojait
Rangpur	Rangpur sadar	Darshana	Ghagot para
Rangpur	Rangpur sadar	Pashuram	Dhap (part-b)
Rangpur	Rangpur sadar	Satgara	Deodoba
Rangpur	Rangpur sadar	Tapodhan	Kartik
Rangpur	Rangpur sadar	Ward no-07	Ganeshpur
Rangpur	Rangpur sadar	Ward no-09	Tatipara
Rangpur	Taraganj	Kursha	Ghanirampur
Rangpur	Taraganj	Kursha	Palashbari

Source: Authors' compilation.

Table A.2: Village Census and Sample Households Selected by District

Geographical Units	Dinajpur		Gaibandha		Kurigram		Lalmonirhat		Rangpur		All Districts	
Upazilla	11		7		6		5		7		36	
Union	25		25		20		24		24		118	
Village	26		26		20		26		26		124	
Household type	Sample Frame	Sample	Sample Frame	Sample	Sample Frame	Sample	Sample Frame	Sample	Sample Frame	Sample	Sample Frame	Sample
GB, BRAC, and ASA households combined	2,400	287	1,721	310	1,262	241	1,926	305	2,067	303	9,376	1,446
Other program households	641	0	835	0	435	0	629	0	749	0	3,289	0
Household eligible and willing to participate	620	168	405	171	672	143	341	172	416	177	2,454	831
Household ineligible and willing to participate	309	100	98	65	121	60	135	73	83	57	746	355
Household not willing to Participate	1,241	70	1,950	79	1,419	59	2,128	78	1,886	75	8,624	361
All households	5,211	625	5,009	625	3,909	503	5,159	628	5,201	612	24,489	2993

GB = Grameen Bank.

Source: Authors' calculations based on the ADB–BIDS Digital Microcredit Survey 2021.

Definitions of Different Categories of Industries

Large Industry

In manufacturing, large industry will be deemed to comprise enterprises with either the value (replacement cost) of fixed assets excluding land and building in excess of Tk300 million or with more than 250 workers. For services, large industry will correspond to enterprises with either the value (replacement cost) of fixed assets excluding land and building in excess of Tk150 million or with more than 100 workers.

Medium Industry

In manufacturing, medium industry will be deemed to comprise enterprises with either the value (replacement cost) of fixed assets excluding land and building between Tk100 million and Tk300 million, or with between 100 and 250 workers. For services, medium industry will correspond to enterprises with either the value (replacement cost) of fixed assets excluding land and building between Tk10 million and Tk150 million, or with between 50 and 100 workers. If on one criterion, a firm falls into the medium category, while it falls into the large category based on the other criterion, the firm will be deemed to be in the large category.

Small Industry

In manufacturing, small industry will be deemed to comprise enterprises with either the value (replacement cost) of fixed assets excluding land and building between Tk5 million and Tk100 million, or with between 25 and 99 workers. For services, small industry will correspond to enterprises with either the value (replacement cost) of fixed assets excluding land and building between Tk500,000 and Tk10 million, or with between 10 and 25 workers. If on one criterion, a firm falls into the small category, while it falls into the medium category based on the other criterion, the firm will be deemed as in the medium category.

Micro Industry

In manufacturing, micro industry will be deemed to comprise enterprises with either the value (replacement cost) of fixed assets excluding land and building between Tk500,000 and Tk5 million, or with between 10 and 24, or smaller number of, workers. If on one criterion, a firm falls into the micro category, while it falls into the small category based on the other criterion, the firm will be deemed as in the small category.

Cottage Industry

In manufacturing, cottage industry will be deemed to comprise enterprises with either the value (replacement cost) of fixed assets excluding land and building of less than Tk500,000, or with up to nine workers, including household members. If on one criterion, a firm falls into the cottage category, while it falls into the micro category based on the other criterion, the firm will be deemed as in the micro category. A district-wise distribution of industry categories is shown in **Table A.3**.

Table A.3: Distribution of Districtwide Establishment Category, Poverty Headcount Ratio, and Microfinance Regulatory Authority Count

Zila Name	Cottage Industry	Micro Industry	Small Industry	Medium Industry	Large Industry	Poverty Head-Count Ratio	District-Wise MRA Count
BAGERHAT	88.0%	0.6%	11.3%	0.0%	0.0%	31.00	263
BANDARBAN	80.8%	1.5%	17.4%	0.2%	0.1%	63.20	26
BARGUNA	92.7%	1.4%	5.8%	0.1%	0.0%	25.70	163
BARISAL	87.6%	1.0%	11.3%	0.1%	0.0%	27.40	373
BHOLA	91.1%	0.8%	8.0%	0.1%	0.0%	15.50	228
BOGRA	91.4%	1.0%	7.5%	0.1%	0.0%	27.20	651
BRAHMANBARIA	87.8%	1.2%	10.9%	0.0%	0.0%	10.30	358
CHANDPUR	85.5%	1.4%	13.1%	0.1%	0.0%	29.30	350
CHAPAI NABABGANJ	86.5%	0.9%	12.5%	0.1%	0.0%	39.60	351
CHITTAGONG	79.3%	1.5%	18.9%	0.1%	0.2%	13.70	1045
CHUADANGA	85.1%	0.6%	14.3%	0.1%	0.0%	31.90	281
COMILLA	87.0%	1.4%	11.4%	0.1%	0.0%	16.60	872
COXS BAZAR	86.4%	0.8%	12.7%	0.1%	0.0%	13.50	243
DHAKA	70.1%	2.4%	27.0%	0.3%	0.2%	10.00	1467
DINAJPUR	97.0%	0.5%	2.4%	0.0%	0.0%	64.30	604
FARIDPUR	95.1%	0.6%	4.3%	0.1%	0.0%	7.70	374
FENI	88.8%	1.3%	9.8%	0.1%	0.0%	8.10	242
GAIBANDHA	97.4%	0.4%	2.1%	0.0%	0.0%	46.70	321
GAZIPUR	86.0%	1.2%	12.3%	0.2%	0.4%	6.90	670
GOPALGANJ	95.4%	0.6%	4.0%	0.0%	0.0%	29.50	195
HABIGANJ	91.2%	1.1%	7.6%	0.0%	0.0%	13.40	193
JAMALPUR	96.8%	0.4%	2.8%	0.0%	0.0%	52.50	192
JESSORE	93.1%	0.8%	5.9%	0.1%	0.1%	26.90	566
JHALOKATI	95.6%	0.5%	3.8%	0.1%	0.0%	21.50	91
JHENAIDAH	95.2%	0.7%	4.0%	0.1%	0.0%	26.50	398
JOYPURHAT	94.7%	1.0%	4.2%	0.0%	0.0%	21.40	207
KHAGRACHHARI	90.7%	1.2%	7.8%	0.1%	0.1%	52.70	62
KHULNA	89.9%	1.0%	8.9%	0.1%	0.1%	30.80	449
KISHOREGONJ	93.2%	1.0%	5.7%	0.1%	0.0%	53.50	349
KURIGRAM	97.6%	0.3%	2.1%	0.0%	0.0%	70.80	233
KUSHTIA	94.3%	0.9%	4.7%	0.0%	0.0%	17.50	437
LAKSHMIPUR	97.6%	0.3%	2.0%	0.0%	0.0%	32.50	240
LALMONIRHAT	51.5%	9.5%	39.0%	0.0%	0.0%	42.00	161
MADARIPUR	93.6%	0.8%	5.5%	0.1%	0.0%	3.70	194

continued on next page

Table A.3 continued

Zila Name	Cottage Industry	Micro Industry	Small Industry	Medium Industry	Large Industry	Poverty Head-Count Ratio	District-Wise MRA Count
MAGURA	89.5%	0.5%	9.9%	0.0%	0.0%	56.70	188
MANIKGANJ	89.7%	1.3%	8.9%	0.1%	0.1%	30.70	321
MAULVIBAZAR	83.7%	1.4%	14.9%	0.0%	0.0%	11.00	176
MEHERPUR	90.1%	0.6%	9.2%	0.1%	0.0%	31.50	147
MUNSHIGANJ	84.5%	1.8%	13.4%	0.2%	0.1%	3.10	275
MYMENSINGH	90.2%	0.4%	9.3%	0.0%	0.0%	22.00	447
NAOGAON	90.6%	0.7%	8.6%	0.1%	0.0%	32.20	576
NARAIL	88.7%	0.6%	10.6%	0.0%	0.0%	16.80	100
NARAYANGANJ	81.0%	3.1%	15.2%	0.3%	0.3%	2.60	487
NARSINGDI	81.2%	2.4%	16.2%	0.1%	0.1%	10.50	348
NATORE	88.0%	0.9%	11.0%	0.1%	0.0%	24.00	336
NETRAKONA	91.1%	0.7%	8.2%	0.1%	0.0%	34.00	216
NILPHAMARI	69.9%	5.2%	24.8%	0.0%	0.0%	32.30	277
NOAKHALI	91.0%	0.4%	8.6%	0.1%	0.0%	23.30	412
PABNA	86.7%	2.5%	10.7%	0.1%	0.0%	33.00	543
PANCHAGARH	93.2%	0.3%	6.4%	0.1%	0.0%	26.30	164
PATUAKHALI	95.2%	0.4%	4.3%	0.1%	0.0%	37.20	269
PIROJPUR	89.6%	0.9%	9.4%	0.1%	0.0%	32.20	166
RAJBARI	91.9%	0.5%	7.6%	0.0%	0.0%	33.80	203
RAJSHAHI	88.5%	0.8%	10.6%	0.1%	0.0%	20.10	644
RANGAMATI	84.4%	1.5%	13.9%	0.1%	0.1%	28.50	48
RANGPUR	79.5%	1.9%	18.5%	0.1%	0.0%	43.80	418
SATKHIRA	88.3%	0.7%	10.8%	0.1%	0.0%	18.60	385
SHARIATPUR	89.9%	0.6%	9.5%	0.0%	0.0%	15.70	205
SHERPUR	96.3%	0.5%	3.1%	0.0%	0.0%	41.30	99
SIRAJGANJ	91.2%	3.7%	5.0%	0.1%	0.0%	30.50	431
SUNAMGANJ	95.1%	0.7%	4.1%	0.0%	0.0%	26.00	134
SYLHET	88.2%	0.9%	10.8%	0.1%	0.1%	13.00	187
TANGAIL	94.0%	1.2%	4.7%	0.1%	0.0%	19.00	747
THAKURGAON	96.9%	0.8%	2.2%	0.0%	0.0%	23.40	176

MRA = Microcredit Regulatory Authority.

Note: The definitions under 2.20 are as per the *National Industrial Policy, 2010.*

Source: Government of Bangladesh, Ministry of Industries. The National Industrial Policy, 2010. Dhaka.

Figure A.1: Poverty Map of Bangladesh—Proportion of Population Below Poverty Line by District

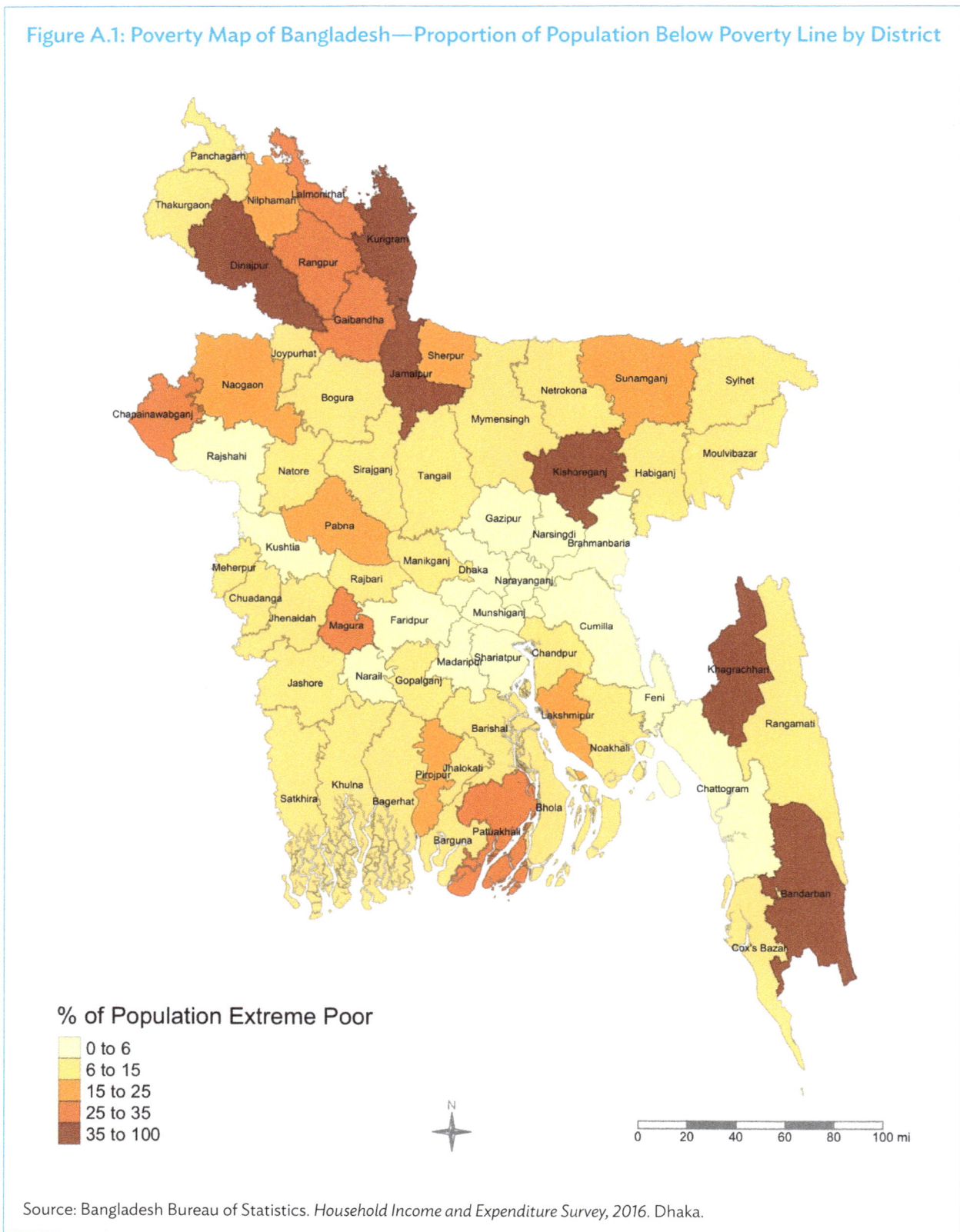

% of Population Extreme Poor

- 0 to 6
- 6 to 15
- 15 to 25
- 25 to 35
- 35 to 100

Source: Bangladesh Bureau of Statistics. *Household Income and Expenditure Survey, 2016.* Dhaka.

Figure A.2: Proportion of Microfinance Institution Count by District

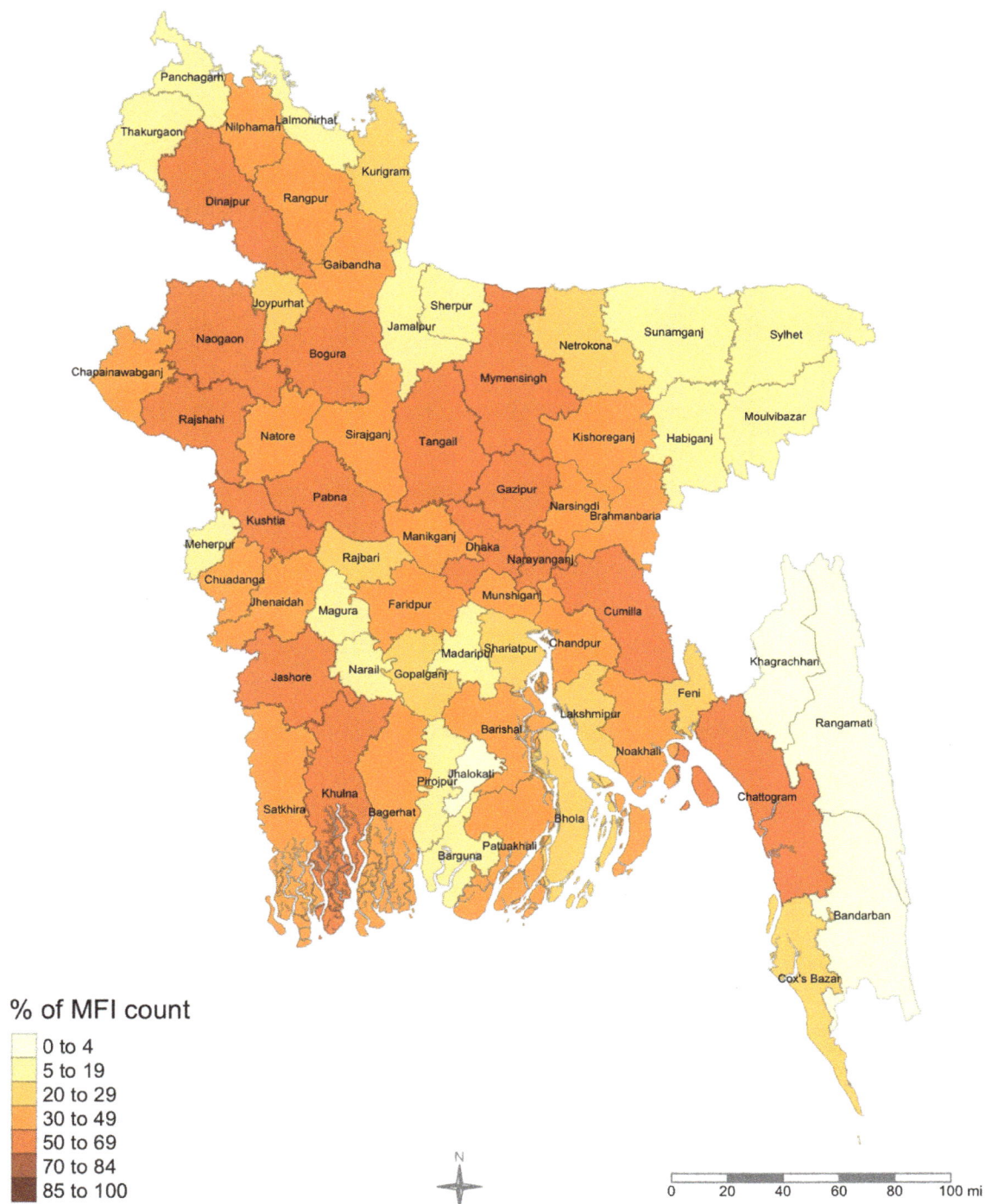

% of MFI count
- 0 to 4
- 5 to 19
- 20 to 29
- 30 to 49
- 50 to 69
- 70 to 84
- 85 to 100

Source: Microcredit Regulatory Authority.

References

Andrianaivo, Mihasonirina, Ilias Skamnelos, and Aminata Ndiaye. 2019. *Financing Solutions for Micro, Small, and Medium Enterprises in Bangladesh*. Finance. World Bank.

Asian Development Bank (ADB). 2021. *Asia Small and Medium-Sized Enterprise Monitor 2021: Volume I–Country and Regional Reviews*. Manila: ADB.

Aterido, Reyes, Mary Hallward-Driemeier, and Carmen Pagés. 2011. "Big Constraints to Small Firms' Growth? Business Environment and Employment Growth across Firms," *Economic Development and Cultural Change* 59 (3): 609–47.

Badruddoza, Syed. 2013. "Rules of Microcredit Regulatory Authority in Bangladesh: A Synopsis." *MPRA Working Paper* No. 44637. https://mpra.ub.uni-muenchen.de/44637/.

Bangladesh Bank. 2021. Bangladesh Bank. Payment Systems. https://www.bb.org.bd/fnansys/regulator.php Bangladesh Bureau of Statistics. *Household Income and Expenditure Survey, 2011–2019/20*. Dhaka.

———. 2013. *Economic Census*. Dhaka.

Banerjee, Abhijit, and Esther Duflo. 2005. "Growth Theory through the Lens of Development Economics." In *Handbook of Economic Growth Edition 1, Volume 1*, edited by Philippe Aghion and Steven Durlauf, 473–552.

Beck, Thorsten, Asli Demiraguc-Kunt, and Patrick Honohan. 2006. "Access to Financial Services: Measurement, Impact, and Policy." World Bank (mimeo).

Beck, Thorsten, Asli Demirgüc-Kunt, and Vojislav Maksimovic. 2005. "Financial and Legal Constraints to Growth: Does Firm Size Matter?" *Journal of Finance* 60 (1):131–77.

Business Finance for the Poor in Bangladesh. 2017. *Diagnostics of Microenterprise Lending by MFIs in Bangladesh: Opportunities and Challenges*. http://inm.org.bd/wp-content/uploads/2017/07/Policy-Brief_ME_English.pdf.

Butler, Alexander, and Jess Cornaggia. 2011. "Does Access to External Finance Improve Productivity? Evidence from a Natural Experiment." *Journal of Financial Economics* 99 (1): 184–203.

Buyinza, Faisal, and Edward Bbaale. 2013. "Access to Credit and the Effect of Credit Constraints on the Performance of Manufacturing Firms in the East African Region: Micro Analysis." *International Journal of Economics and Finance* 5 (10): 85–99.

Caselli, Francesco, and James Freyer. 2007. "The Marginal Product of Capital," *Quarterly Journal of Economics* 122 (2): 535–68.

Credit and Development Forum. *Bangladesh Micro Finance Statistics, 2011 to 2019/20*. Dhaka.

Cull, Robert, and Lixin Colin Xu. 2005. "Institutions, Ownership, and Finance: The Determinants of Profit Reinvestment Among Chinese Firms." *Journal of Financial Economics* 77 (1): 117–46.

de Mel, Suresh, David McKenzie, and Christopher Woodruff. 2008. "Returns to Capital in Microenterprises: Evidence from a Field Experiment." *Quarterly Journal of Economics* 123 (4): 1329–72.

Deininger, Klaus, and Songqing Jin. 2007. "Securing Property Rights in Transition: Lessons from Implementation of China's Rural Land Contracting Law." *World Bank Policy Research Working Paper* No. 4447.

Government of Bangladesh, Ministry of Industries. The National Industrial Policy, 2010. Dhaka.

Iqbal, Kazi, Kazi Toufique, Nazneen Ahmed, Nahid Pabon, and Wahid Ibon. 2019. "Dynamics of Rural Nonfarm Sector: 2000–2016." Bangladesh Institute of Development Studies (mimeo).

Khalily, Baqui, and Abdul Khaleque. 2018. "The Effects of Access to Credit on Productivity of Microenterprises: An Empirical Evidence from Bangladesh." *International Journal of SME Development* 4 (2018): 1–40.

Khandker, Shahidur. 2021. "Credit for Agricultural Developmen.t" In *Agricultural Development: New Perspectives in a Changing World*, edited by K. Otsuka and S. Fan, International Food Policy Research Institute: Washington, DC.

Khandker, Shahidur, Baqui Khalily, and Hussain Samad. 2016. *Beyond Ending Poverty: The Dynamics of Microfinance in Bangladesh*. World Bank, Washington, DC.

Khandker, Shahidur, Hussain Samad, and Rubaba Ali. 2014. "Does Access to Finance Matter in Microenterprise Growth? Evidence from Bangladesh." World Bank (mimeo).

Maddala, G.S. 1983. *Limited-Dependent Qualitative Variables in Econometrics*. Cambridge, United Kingdom: Cambridge University Press.

Murshid, K.A.S., Shahidur Khandker, Khondoker Shakhawat Ali, Hussain Samad, and Monzur Hossain. 2020. *Impact of Mobile Financial Services in Bangladesh: The Case of bKash*, Bangladesh Institute of Development Studies: Dhaka.

Rand, John. 2007. "Credit Constraints and Determinants of the Cost of Capital in Vietnamese Manufacturing." *Small Business Economics* 29 (1): 1–13.

Sawada, Naotaka, and Jian Zhang. 2012. "Promoting the Rural Farm and Nonfarm Businesses Evidence from the Yemen Rural Investment Climate." *World Bank Policy Research Working Paper* No. 6128.

World Bank. 2007. "Bangladesh: Strategy for Sustained Growth" *Bangladesh Development Series Paper* No. 18. World Bank, Dhaka.

———. 2019. "Bangladesh: Seizing the Opportunity." *World Bank Policy Notes*. Washington, DC.

Zinman, Jonathan. 2002. "The Efficacy and Efficiency of Credit Market Interventions: Evidence from the Community Reinvestment Act." Joint Center for Housing Studies of Harvard University.

www.ingramcontent.com/pod-product-compliance
Lightning Source LLC
Chambersburg PA
CBHW061221270326
41926CB00032B/4796